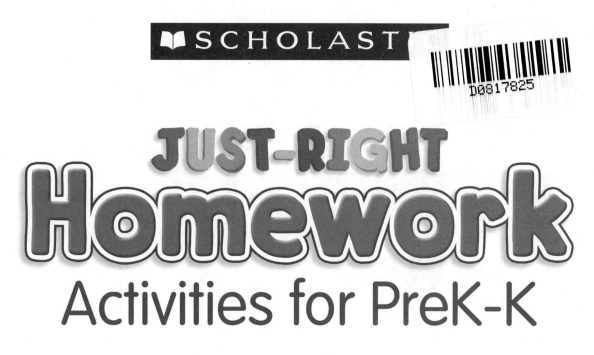

JUST-RIGHT Homework
Activities for PreK-K

50+ Quick and Easy Send-Home Activities for Building Early Reading and Math Skills

Deborah Diffily
& Charlotte Sassman

New York • Toronto • London • Auckland • Sydney
Mexico City • New Delhi • Hong Kong • Buenos Aires

Teaching *Resources*

To our editor, Maria Chang

Thank you, Maria, for your patience, guidance, and expertise.
Above all, we appreciate and thank you for your always unfailing
cheerfulness and gracious spirit. You're the best!

Editor: Maria L. Chang

Cover design by Jason Robinson

Cover photograph © Image Source

Interior design by Holly Grundon

Interior illustrations by Maxie Chambliss, Paige Billin-Frye, Shelley Dieterichs,
    James Graham Hale, Jason Robinson, Rusty Fletcher, Mike Moran

ISBN-13: 978-0-439-91225-9

ISBN-10: 0-439-91225-3

Contents

I. Math

A. Knowing Numbers

B. Counting

C. Patterns

D. Sorting

E. Solving Problems

II. Reading and Writing

D. Phonological Awareness

E. Decoding

F. Reading Comprehension

G. Writing Development

III. Alphabet and Numeral Activities

Introduction

Many young children need more academic experiences than we can provide for them. No matter how effective or how well organized you are as a classroom teacher, you can never create more hours in the school day. And yet, as early childhood educators, we know that most young children need lots of repetition with early literacy and mathematical concepts before they commit them to long-term memory.

One of the best ways for expanding school learning is to extend that learning into our students' homes. But "homework" has negative connotations for lots of different reasons.

In one of his poems, Shel Silverstein discusses the invention of a "homework machine," expressing for many the almost universal dislike of homework. Not only do students perceive homework as something to avoid, but these days, many families realistically have little time to complete it. This book seeks to address both issues and to change homework attitudes by offering children and teachers meaningful alternatives to homework "drudgery."

Research shows that a child needs to practice a new skill many times to fully learn it. Teachers and families alike accept that repetition is necessary. But traditional homework practices of multiple skill-and-drill worksheets are not the only choice. There is no reason that practicing literacy and math skills has to be drudgery. For young children, many of these skills can be practiced in the context of games or other enjoyable activities easily carried out with a family member. This book offers a variety of "family homework" choices that are appropriate for young children and engage both families and children in meaningful, educational, and enjoyable activities.

Using Research-Based Strategies for Homework

Have specific expectations.

Most families want to support their children's learning, but often do not know exactly what they should do. When you send activities home, let families know how much support they should give their children. How should they handle mistakes that their children make in this type of homework? How much time should be spent doing homework? What should families do if the child does not want to do the homework? Research indicates that giving sufficient explanation about expectations boosts homework completion and student learning.

Target homework assignments.

Teachers often send home the same homework for every child in the class. Sometimes this may be a good idea; however, most of the time, different children in a class need to practice different kinds of skills. Research shows that when homework is matched to a student's skills, it more effectively supports his or her learning.

Acknowledge when homework has been done.

While it is not necessary to grade activities such as the ones in this book, research shows that students are more likely to complete their homework when there are positive consequences. Whether it is writing a private note to each student who brings in documentation of having done the homework or inviting students who hand in their homework to line up first for recess, such recognition encourages the completion of homework.

How to Use the Activities With Your Students

Each homework activity is designed to be photocopied and sent home as a stand-alone activity. Families are given clear directions on how to engage their child, play the game or complete the activity, and extend their child's learning.

Prior to using any of the activities, we suggest you send home a letter such as the one on page 11. It explains to families how to complete the activities and how you use them (or similar activities) in the classroom. It also offers them support as they begin to work with their child at home.

Referring to these activities in your regular family communications is also helpful. For example, after the Counting Cars activity (page 23), a typical blurb for your weekly family communication letter might read:

Sample Family Letter

In last week's Counting Cars activity, the results ranged widely. Catherine's street had a slow day, as she reported counting three cars (one blue and one white) and "one really big truck." Lakayia counted the most cars, with 15 going past her house. Bonnie, Carol, and Joan all reported seeing three trucks. But Kyle's observations left the other boys wanting to move to his street. Because of construction on his street, his observations included "one road grader and one roller truck."

Adding Your Personal Touch to the Activities

You always have the option of tailoring these activities to your classroom and particular situation. Adding something meaningful from your class's experience increases the impact of the homework assignment tenfold. Here are some suggestions for personalizing the activities:

❖ Include a paragraph or two describing how you use this activity in the classroom. Mention names of children from your class and/or describe their interactions. For example, when sending the Counting the House homework (page 21), you might include a story or two that come out of a class activity:

This morning in class, we counted the number of windows in our classroom. The children discovered, with my help, that there are six windows in the room, but if you count the tops and bottoms separately, then there are twelve. The class practiced counting the six windows several times. While we were in the lunchroom, Vic excitedly announced, "Miss Kindle, me and Walter have been counting. There are only three windows in here." No only did Vic remember our lesson about counting, but he extended it by noticing that there were fewer windows in the lunchroom.

❖ Mention specific books that you use in the classroom. Families may take their children to the library or bookstore, but often do not know what titles to select. Offering specific suggestions is helpful to them.

✤ Include artwork or samples of children's work. Typically families have no idea what level of work they should expect from their child. Often, when adults help with homework, they focus on things that are most evident, such as tidy handwriting or spelling words correctly. If you send home a sample of an average student's work, this will allow families to see the type of work you expect from children this age.

Setting a Structure for Homework Time

Offer families suggestions on how to structure the homework time. These include time limits, a schedule for homework, and where to complete the activities. Suggest that the homework time should last about 20 minutes. Tell parents that if the homework is taking longer, they can stop and complete it at another time. Encourage them to write you a note if homework is taking too long and offer to help them or their child as needed. Reiterate to them that you will send homework on a specified schedule. You might send homework on Monday and expect a reply by Friday. Other teachers find that sending the week's activity on Friday to be completed by the following Friday gives busy families the weekend to work on it. Finally, suggest that they find a quiet spot where the family can focus on the activity. For each family this area will probably be different. For some, it may be in the family room, and for others, on the floor or in the kitchen. What is important is that they are developing a homework routine that their child can understand and continue to use throughout the grades.

Helping busy families understand the importance of homework and showing them ways to accomplish this task are well worth your time. Your students will benefit, and so will you.

Dear Family:

Young children need many, many experiences with the basic skills of reading, writing, and math before they become competent in these important academic areas. We will be practicing these skills at school, but it is important for children to see these skills as important things to learn, not just "school" things. The more repetition children get with these skills, the sooner they are likely to remember them.

From time to time, I will be sending home a game or other activity, like the attached activity, that supports your child's learning. I ask that you watch for these activities and set aside some time to complete them with your child.

These activities are designed to be short, taking up only about 10 to 20 minutes. Try to build an atmosphere of exploration and joy during this time. Did you know that research shows that we actually learn more when we are in a good mood?

I'll send a homework form with each activity. Please sign the form and return it along with your comments. I'd love to hear what you thought about the activity. This will let me know that you received the activity and spent some time doing it with your child.

I am looking forward to working with you to make this a special year of learning for your child.

Sincerely,

Homework Form

Name: _____

Date: _____

Name of Activity: _____

Comments: _____

_____

_____

_____

Circle the face that best describes your child's learning from this activity:

☺　　　😐　　　☹

We completed this activity on: _____

Signature _____

Introduction to Math Homework

The math activities in the following section are designed to do two things. The first is to give young children opportunities to practice the math skills that enable them to become good mathematicians. The second is to involve families in their children's education. Both goals are important to young children's development of mathematical concepts.

For many parents, mathematics in the early grades focused on memorizing addition and subtraction facts. As a result, they have a tendency to create a set of flash cards: 1 + 1 = ___, 1 + 2 = ___, and so on. Then they set about getting their child to memorize the entire stack of cards. This is not particularly engaging to young children, and it is not the best way to lay a good math foundation for them. Memorizing a set of disconnected facts doesn't lead to a deep understanding of how numbers work or how they relate to one another. Today, we want students to arrive at the facts by understanding and applying sound mathematical concepts and patterns, rather than by memorizing them. This is not to say children won't use some memorization at some point to learn the facts, but they should do so only after they develop the sense of numbers.

While children are engaged in the activities in this book, they are practicing and developing important math skills, such as one-to-one correspondence, numeral recognition, sorting skills, patterning skills, and set recognition. Unlike worksheets, these learning experiences keep children active. Unlike "doing homework" off in a corner alone, doing these activities involves family members and reinforces the nature of social learning. These activities help children really experience math concepts. "Experiencing math is more beneficial than straight learning," says Cathy Seeley, former president of the National Council of Teachers of Mathematics. "It stays with kids longer."

Number Go Fish

Targeted skill

Young children are expected to use language to describe the relative size of numbers and to quickly recognize the numerals 0 to 9. Children are also expected to use numbers to describe how many objects are in a set.

Materials

◆ Number Go Fish cards

What to do

This activity is played like the traditional Go Fish game. As your child learns to play, it can be played with two players, but the game is better suited for three or four players.

To play:

1. Shuffle the cards and deal four cards to each player. Stack the remaining cards facedown in the "pond," which is in the center of the playing area.

2. After all players have arranged their hands, play begins. Players place any matches faceup on the table. Players replace those cards by drawing additional cards from the pond.

3. Player 1 asks Player 2 for a card that matches one that is in his hand. If Player 2 has that card, she gives it to Player 1 and draws a card from the pond. If the desired card is unavailable, Player 2 says, "Go fish," and Player 1 draws a card from the pond.

4. The first player to match all his or her cards wins the game.

Just-Right Homework Activities for PreK–K © 2009 by Diffily & Sassman, Scholastic Teaching Resources

Number Go Fish *(continued)*

Extending the activity

❖ To make the game more challenging, deal more cards to each player at the start of the game.

❖ You can make additional game cards to require a match of three or four cards, to accommodate more players, or to include the numbers 11 to 20.

❖ This activity helps your child associate a numeral's name with its shape and form. At first, your child may have difficulty remembering the names of the numerals. If so, write them in order from zero to nine on a piece of paper. Encourage your child to use this paper to count to find the name of the needed numeral.

❖ Show your child how to arrange his or her hand. Explain how to begin the game by putting the cards in numerical order to find cards that match and to make cards easier to find as the game progresses.

❖ If holding the cards is uncomfortable for your child, show how to place the cards facedown in front of him or her. Or, if you're playing at a table, your child can place his or her cards on an empty chair.

❖ Provide some small objects and ask your child to show you what card he or she wants by counting out that many objects. For example, if your child desires a match for a 4, then he or she would count out four objects and place them in the playing area. You can recount the objects and give your child the needed card (or say "go fish").

❖ Use this opportunity to practice the good manners required in game playing, such as asking for a card in a polite way, being a gracious winner (or loser), and taking turns.

More questions to ask

As you play, talk about the value of the numbers. You might say, "Oh, you asked me for a 4. Let's see, that is more than three. Yes, here's a 4 for your match." Use mathematical terms such as *larger*, *smaller*, *more than* or *greater than*, *less than*, *match*, and *equal*.

What your child is practicing

Your child is not only learning mathematical language and concepts, but he or she is also practicing fair play.

Number Go Fish Cards

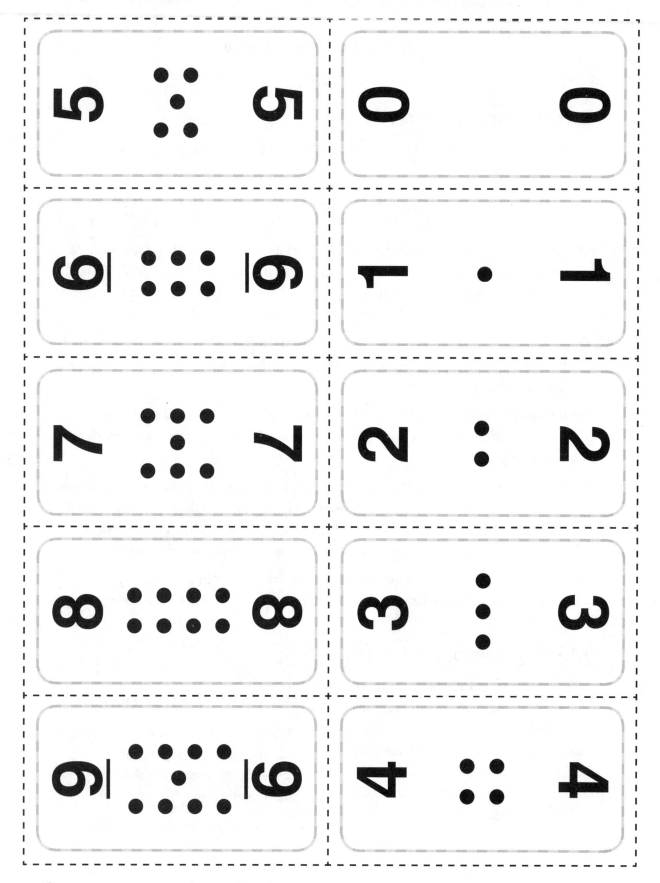

Number Go Fish Cards

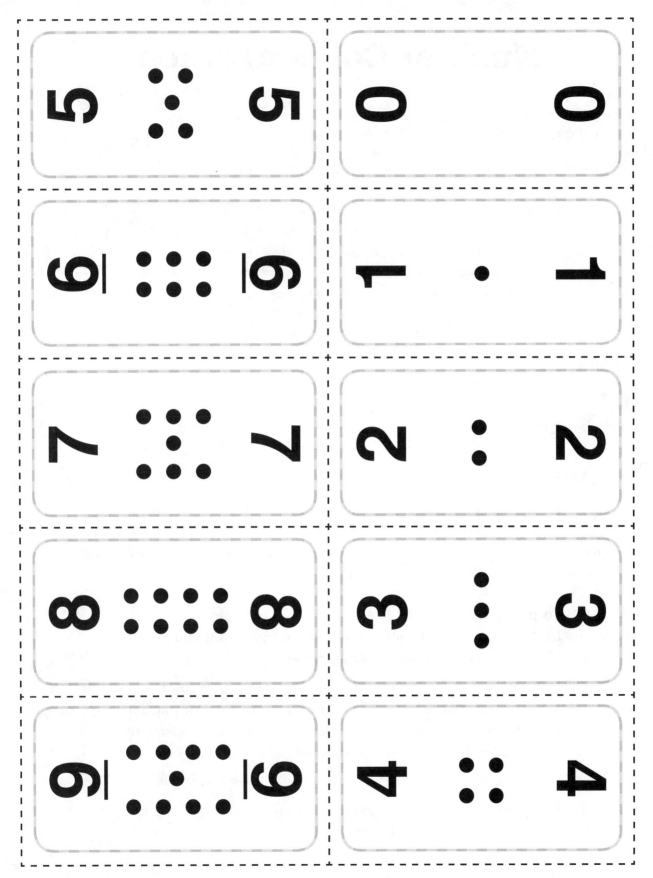

Number Concentration

Targeted skill

Remembering how the lines go together to form a numeral is hard for young children. It is especially hard when more than one arrangement of lines makes the same numeral, as in 4 and 4. Just a small difference of a slanted line meeting a straight one at the top or two straight lines pointing up can indicate totally different numerals to children. Be consistent in how you form the numerals in the beginning, and then show your child the variations as his or her confidence increases.

Materials

♦ index cards

♦ felt-tip markers

What to do

This game is a simpler version of the commercially available games of Memory or Concentration. On index cards write the numerals 0, 1, 2, 3, 4, 5, 6, 7, 8, 9. Create two groups of identical cards. Be sure to form the numerals the same way that your child sees them written at school.

To play:

1. Pick three of the numerals that your child is familiar with and place those pairs facedown on the playing surface.

2. Challenge your child to turn over one card at a time, searching for the two cards that match. When your child finds a matching pair, compliment him or her on the match and repeat the name of that pair, saying, "Yes, those cards both have a 2 on them."

3. Remove the pairs from the playing area until all matches are made.

4. As your child learns the names of more numerals, add more cards to the game until he or she has learned to recognize them all.

Number Concentration (continued)

Extending the activity

✤ Use this game to help your child learn how to form the numerals as well. Encourage him or her to use a finger to trace the numerals you have written on the cards, starting at the top of each form. For example, say, "Yes, you make a 2 by starting at the top, curving around to zoom to the bottom, then slide to the right. That's how you write a 2."

✤ Provide pencil and paper with large lines to encourage your child to practice writing the numerals. Lightly write it for him or her to trace at first. Then encourage him or her to form the numerals independently.

✤ Young children often benefit from "feeling the shape" of a numeral. Write the numerals on index cards and trace the numerals with glue. When they're dry, your child can trace their raised shapes to help him or her learn to write the numerals.

✤ Raise your child's understanding of what numerals represent by pointing them out when you see them in the real world. Note the numerals used to show the price of gasoline at the gas station or the price signs in the produce section of the grocery store. Point out numerals on billboards or other large signs you see from the car or on the cash register as you pay for items.

More questions to ask

As your child's knowledge increases, ask him or her questions about the value of each numeral. For example, "Yes, those are 4s. Is a 4 bigger or smaller than the 6s you just found?"

What your child is practicing

It takes lots of practice to remember the numbers and their names. It is natural for your child to remember some of them more quickly than others. Celebrate the successes and help your child as he or she learns the other numbers.

Reading the Calendar

Targeted skill

Young children become familiar with how the value of numbers increases as they count forward and decreases as they count backward. Phrases such as "two more days" or "that happened three days ago" help them understand this concept.

Materials

♦ calendar with large spaces (A wall-sized calendar works well, but any calendar is appropriate.)

♦ highlighter

What your child is practicing

Your child is learning to count and to associate a value with the written symbol. While this is easy for adults, it is hard for children at first. Discussing events and clearly stating the name of the day helps your child understand the passage of time and how the days relate to each other.

What to do

As events that relate to your child are planned, write them on a calendar. Introduce the names of the days and explain how they make up a week. You might highlight the days in one calendar week, coloring the Sunday to Saturday squares with a light color. As your child gets more familiar with the idea of a week, you can explain how all the squares in one column represent the same day, such as how the second column contains all the Mondays.

Extending the activity

✤ Encourage your child to consult the calendar to see when family events will occur. Be sure the calendar events are meaningful to your child, such as "Go to the park." You can also draw a quick sketch of a park instead of using words.

✤ Encourage your child to count to determine how many days until an event will occur, so he or she will begin to understand counting and the order of numbers.

More questions to ask

Asking the questions "how many more?" or "how many fewer?" helps your child understand the ideas of adding and subtracting. Showing your child these concepts on the calendar helps your child form a visual picture in his or her mind, making them easier to understand.

Counting the House

Targeted skill

Young children are learning to associate a numeral, such as 4 or 2, with that number of objects; for example, four blocks or two dogs.

What to do

Using familiar objects makes learning to count more meaningful for your child. Challenge your child to count the windows in your house. Then walk through the house with your child and point to each window, helping your child keep count.

Extending the activity

✤ Write down the numeral that represents the number of objects you counted. Keep a journal, "Objects in Our House." On each page, have your child write (or draw) the object and write the numeral that represents how many of them there are in your house. Don't forget to count items in your kitchen (forks, knives, spoons, plates, cups, glasses), garage (screwdrivers, gardening tools, wrenches), pantry (cans, bottles, sodas), bedroom (stuffed animals, books, shirts, pants), and so on.

✤ Your child can make number labels for each object. Have your child create a series of number cards, with a numeral on each one. Then he or she attaches the 1 card to the first object counted, the 2 card to the second object, and so on.

Counting the House *(continued)*

✤ If your child finds it confusing to keep track of what number comes next, gather a handful of small objects (for example, beans, cubes, blocks) to use for counting. For each window your child finds, he or she can take one of the beans as a counter. After all of the windows have been identified, you and your child can count the number of beans. Also, you can use a different counter for each room, such as beans for the windows in the bedroom, cubes for windows in the living room, and so on. Then you can determine a total for the number of windows in the house.

✤ Take advantage of any opportunity to count. For example, when you are in the car or walking down the street, ask your child to count the number of houses (or front steps, trees, dogs) you pass. When you are in line at a fast-food restaurant, ask him or her to count the number of people in line and so on.

More questions to ask

As your child gets better at counting, ask him or her to make predictions about the number of objects around you. For example, if he or she counts five people in line, ask how many legs (or ears, eyes, noses) those people have. Extend this conversation to explore other groupings of numbers, for example, "If there were two cows in a field, how many legs would there be?" Help your child make connections among numbers in this way.

What your child is practicing

Understanding that numbers have an assigned value can be a hard concept for young children, as is the concept of "one more" or "one less." Practicing these ideas (and repeating them over and over) helps your child make these connections.

Just-Right Homework Activities for PreK–K © 2009 by Diffily & Sassman, Scholastic Teaching Resources

Counting Cars

Targeted skill

Young children are expected to record and explain observations using objects, words, pictures, and numbers. As they learn probability and statistics, they are expected to construct graphs using real objects and to use information from a graph to answer questions.

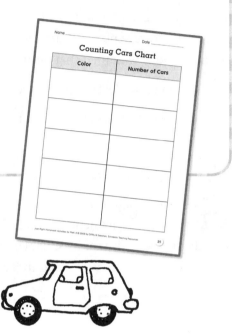

Materials

- Counting Cars Chart
- pencil or other writing tool
- clipboard (or other hard surface)
- timer (or watch)

What to do

Help your child set up the chart by identifying the most common colors for cars in your area. List these on the left column of the chart. (It may help younger children to write the name of each color with a marker of that color or to make a color swatch next to the name.) As you observe cars that pass by, help your child make a tally mark in the proper place to represent each car's color. Observe for a given length of time (five minutes for younger children, ten for older ones).

Discuss the results with your child. Determine the colors with the greatest and least number of cars and whether any colors had an equal number of cars. Determine the total number of cars observed.

Counting Cars (continued)

Extending the activity

✤ Encourage your child to make predictions about how the results would differ if the activity were conducted at a different time of day or in a different place. Compare these predictions with the actual results.

✤ Help your child write simple statements to summarize the results.

✤ Note other things that commonly pass by a given area and count them as well.

More questions to ask

Help your child make reasonable predictions related to this activity. Often making a "reasonable" prediction or statement is tricky for young children. As your child makes a prediction, ask, "Is that reasonable?" Accept the explanation, but after the observation time is completed ask your child to reevaluate the reasonableness of the prediction.

What your child is practicing

Your child is not only practicing necessary math skills, but also learning to patiently work through a task until it is completed.

Name _____ Date _____

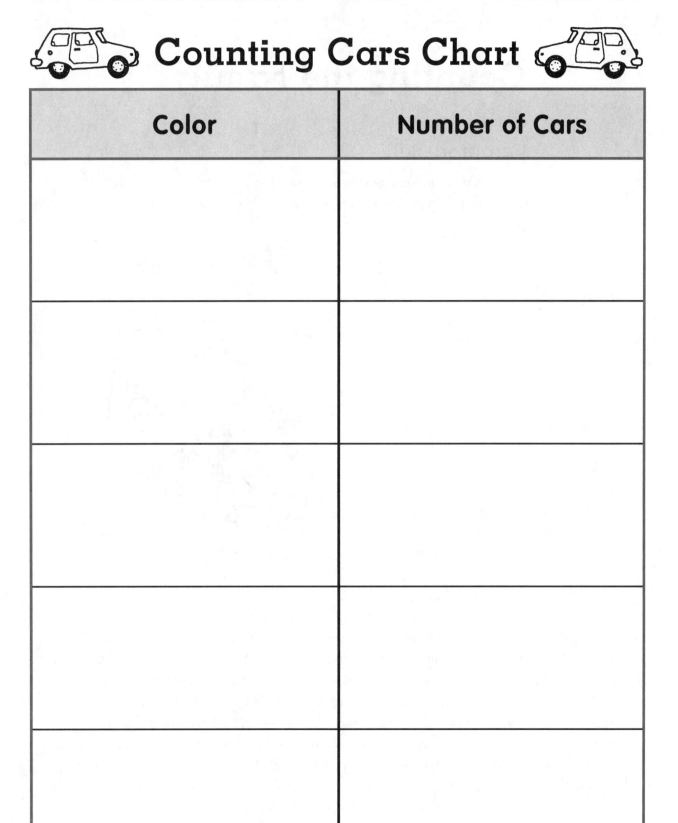 Counting Cars Chart

Color	Number of Cars

Counting the Family

Targeted skill

Young children are expected to count objects and associate that number with the objects it represents.

Materials

♦ paper

♦ pen, pencil, crayon, felt-tip marker, or other writing tool

♦ family's personal items, such as clothing

What to do

This activity is not so much a game as a way of making counting a part of everyday life at home. Young children need lots of opportunities to simply count things. Introduce the idea of "taking inventory," as clerks do in stores. Ask your child to help you take inventory of the family's clothing. Count everyone's socks one day, shoes the next. Count T-shirts, underwear, jeans, shirts, and so on. This gives children a reason to count things. When young children feel they are doing something to help the family, they take the idea more seriously.

For example, if you and your child are taking inventory of the family's socks, you might begin in your child's room, with the sock drawer. Place all of the socks on the bed. Help your child count the pairs (or you can count individual socks if you wish) as he or she returns them to the drawer. You might also have your child simply move the pairs from one area on the bed to another area as he or she counts. After that, the socks can be returned to the drawer. Then move on to another family member's sock drawer.

As you count things together, record them and talk about larger and smaller numbers. Comparing quantities is another important mathematical skill and is best practiced in the context of doing something the child believes is important.

Counting the Family *(continued)*

Extending the activity

After your child has had multiple opportunities to count things and record them, expand the idea of taking inventory to other things in the house. You can count the number of doors and windows, the number of cans and boxes of food, the number of pots and pans. Or go into your child's room and work with him or her to take inventory of things you find there. Remember to let your child do the actual counting and recording of the numbers of things.

What your child is practicing

As your child counts things, he or she is developing number sense. Just because your child can say the numbers in order doesn't necessarily indicate that he or she truly understands what they mean. When your child counts different things, he or she comes to realize that four spoons is the same amount as four cookies, and five forks is the same amount as five markers. This kind of number sense is an important foundational math skill.

Ordering Numbers

Targeted skill

Young children develop their number sense as they compare numbers and place them in the correct order.

Materials

♦ 10 index cards

♦ pen, pencil, crayon, felt-tip marker, or other writing tool

What to do

Write the numerals 0 to 9 on index cards, then shuffle them. Spread the cards faceup on the floor or a large table. Then arrange the cards in the correct order. First, choose the 0 card and place it to the left, choose the 1 card and place it to the right of the 0 card, and so forth, until all the cards are in order. Ask your child to read the cards, pointing to each card and saying the number: "Zero, one, two, three," and so on. Shuffle the cards again and spread them out. This time, ask your child to put the cards in order. After your child has become comfortable with ordering the cards, try giving him or her only a few of the cards, for example, the 3, 4, 6, 7, and 10. Then ask your child to order these.

Extending the activity

✤ After your child can order the cards by starting with 0 and working sequentially, challenge him or her to arrange them in order even if they're out of sequence. That is, shuffle the cards and stack them in the middle of the playing area. Ask your child to turn over the first card, read it, and place it approximately where it belongs. For example, a 7 card should be placed slightly to the right of center. The 3 card should be placed more to the left of center, allowing room for the 4, 5, and 6 cards to go in between.

✤ When your child feels comfortable ordering the cards 0 to 9, begin introducing double-digit numbers up to 20. Repeat the same procedure of having your child put the cards in order many, many times.

✤ When your child is confident with putting all the numbers in order, choose only a few and ask your child to order these. Then ask him or her to figure out which numbers are missing.

What your child is practicing

In this activity, your child simply compares numbers and puts them in the proper order.

Rolling, Rolling, Rolling

Targeted skill

Young children are learning to recognize numbers and understand that numbers can be greater than, less than, or equal to other numbers.

Materials

- ◆ 2 dice
- ◆ counters (cereal, dried beans, buttons)
- ◆ timer

What to do

This game is designed for two players.

To play:

1. Each player has one die.

2. Both players roll their dice at the same time. Then they determine who rolled the greater number. The player who rolled the greater number gets a counter.

3. If both players roll the same number, both take a counter.

4. Play continues for a set amount of time. The player with the most counters at the end is the winner.

Extending the activity

✤ As a variation, the player who rolls the smaller number gets to take the counter. Or instead of taking one counter, the player with the greater number can take the number of counters indicated on the die.

✤ By restating the rolls of the dice and asking questions to compare the amounts, you are reinforcing the concepts of the game. For example, if a 4 and a 2 are rolled, say, "Hey, I rolled a 4 and you rolled a 2! Who rolled the larger number? How much larger is 4 than 2? How much smaller is 2 than 4?" Using math vocabulary (How many more? How many less? Which is larger? Which is smaller? Is ___ greater than or less than ___?) helps your child learn what those terms mean in a fun way.

What your child is practicing

In this game, your child must take turns and correctly evaluate the difference between the individual rolls of the dice. He or she is learning to cooperate and speak to the other player in a respectful voice.

Boy, Girl, Boy, Girl

Targeted skill

Young children are expected to identify, extend, and create patterns using a variety of objects, including concrete objects, sound, and physical movement.

Materials

◆ Patterns for the boy and girl silhouettes (Cut these out for your child or help your child with the task, as appropriate.)

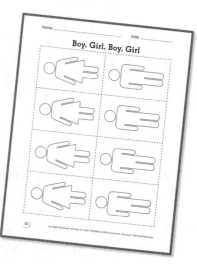

What to do

Lay the silhouettes in front of your child in the order of boy, girl, boy, girl, boy, girl. Leave room at the end of the line for the rest of the shapes. Ask your child to "read" the silhouettes and help him or her say, "Boy, girl, boy, girl, boy, girl." Indicate the next space in the line and ask your child which shape should go there. After encouraging your child to place the "boy" shape there, ask him or her to reread the line of silhouettes. When your child reaches the end of the line, encourage him or her to add the next silhouette and reread the line.

Boy, Girl, Boy, Girl *(continued)*

Extending the activity

❖ Rearrange the silhouettes into other patterns. Begin with boy, boy, girl, boy, boy, girl. Then follow the same process to help your child place the needed silhouettes.

❖ Continue with other patterns such as girl, girl, boy; boy, boy, girl, girl; boy, boy, boy, girl; girl, girl, girl, boy.

❖ Use familiar objects to make patterns. For example, use forks, knives, and spoons from the kitchen to make patterns such as fork, fork, spoon; knife, knife, spoon, spoon; knife, fork, spoon; spoon, spoon, fork, knife.

❖ These patterns can also be labeled in other ways. For example, the pattern of boy, girl, boy, girl can be labeled as ABAB. Assigning a letter to the shape helps your child associate the pattern with an abstract representation.

❖ As a further extension, you can suggest that "two repeats of two objects" makes four objects in the line. This is the basis for addition and multiplication.

❖ You can also use physical movements and sounds to create patterns such as clap, clap, tap or boing, boing, thump.

More questions to ask

Ask your child how many times the pattern repeats. This will encourage him or her to divide the line of objects into smaller parts. For example, four silhouettes arranged boy, girl, boy, girl consist of two repetitions.

What your child is practicing

Practicing arranging objects into patterns helps your child learn to predict. Math calls not only for predicting, but also for making reasonable predictions. This is practiced on a very basic level in this activity. For example, ask your child if it is reasonable that a spoon would appear in a knife, knife, fork pattern. While this may seem funny, it will help your child learn to make reasonable predictions.

Boy, Girl, Boy, Girl

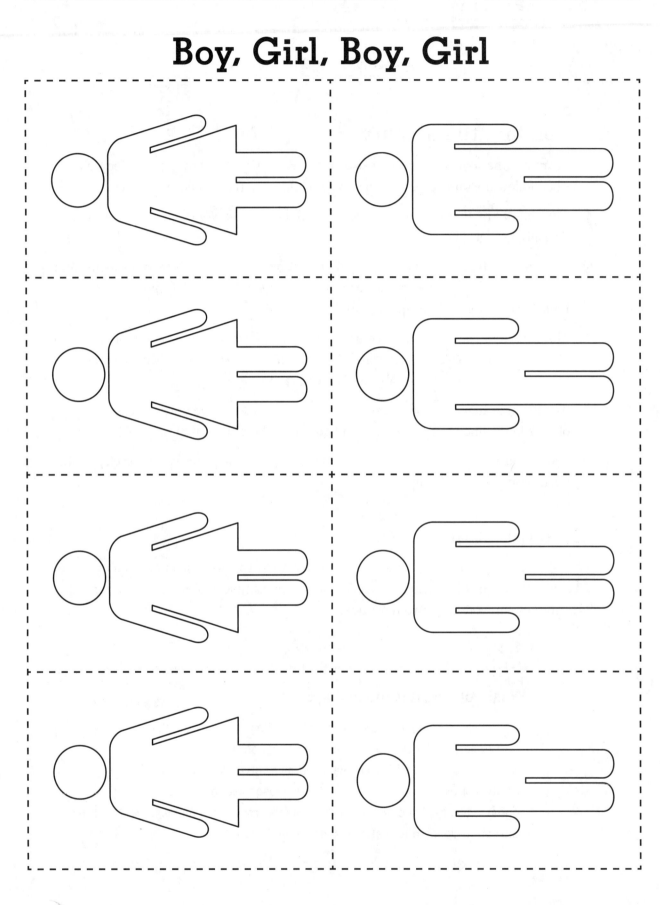

Follow Me

Targeted skill

Young children are expected to identify, extend, and create patterns of sounds, physical movements, and concrete objects. Additionally, they are expected to use the given parts of a pattern to predict what comes next in a sequence.

What to do

This activity helps your child learn to do a series of activities that are repeated in a pattern. Use clapping hands, tapping knees, and snapping fingers to create simple patterns. As your child recognizes the pattern, encourage him or her to follow and extend it.

You might begin by sitting on the floor, facing your child. Clap your hands one time and tap your knees one time, then repeat the sequence until your child can do it with you. Repeat the same ABAB pattern with different motions, such as clap, snap; tap, snap; or snap, clap.

Extending the activity

✤ Ask your child to "name" the pattern, that is, attach words or letters to the pattern to identify it. An ABAB pattern has two elements that alternate. In an AAB pattern, the first action is repeated twice and the second action is repeated once. An ABC pattern involves a sequence of three motions that repeat.

✤ Add motions such as touching your shoulders, crossing arms over your chest, waving hands over your head, touching your head, touching the floor.

✤ Patterns can be created using sound. For example, fill soda bottles with varying levels of water to create different sounds when tapped or gather a variety of bells to ring. Concrete objects such as small blocks, buttons, bottle caps, lids, rocks, and keys can also be used to make patterns.

✤ Asking your child to explain what comes next extends the learning in this activity. Also ask, "What comes before?" or "What if I changed the ____ to ____?" to further extend the learning.

What your child is practicing

Since patterns form the basis of all mathematics, you are helping your child develop a lifelong understanding of mathematical concepts.

Echo Clapping

Targeted skill

Young children are expected to listen to and reproduce patterns and extend them.

What to do

Remind your child about the times you worked together to create patterns and remind him or her that a pattern is something that repeats over and over. Explain that patterns can be clapped, then demonstrate by clapping this pattern: clap [pause] clap clap [long pause]; clap [pause] clap clap [long pause]; clap [pause] clap clap [long pause].

Ask your child to tell you the pattern, allowing him or her a few moments to think of a reply. The correct answer would be one clap followed by two claps.

Try another pattern: clap clap [pause] clap clap clap [long pause]; clap clap [pause] clap clap clap [long pause]; and so on. Ask your child to clap the pattern after you.

Continue with other clapping patterns. If you notice that your child is not grasping the concept of creating patterns by clapping, repeat the above patterns and provide more practice time. If your child understands how to clap patterns, try more complicated ones. Then ask your child to clap a pattern for you (or other family members) to repeat.

Extending the activity

As an extension, find sticks that can be used as drumsticks. Beat patterns on different surfaces (pots and pans, glasses, oatmeal boxes, canned vegetables).

What your child is practicing

Because patterns are a fundamental part of mathematics, it is important for your child to establish a strong foundation of recognizing and extending patterns when he or she is young. Clapping patterns is an activity that can be done virtually anywhere: driving to school, waiting in line at the grocery store, before or after a meal, in the bathtub. It only takes a minute or two, and children really like creating them and extending them into increasingly complicated forms.

Color Patterns

Targeted skill

Young children learn to continue and create various patterns as they complete this activity.

Materials

♦ colored beads, colored blocks, colored adhesive dots, and other suitable items

What to do

Place objects in an AB pattern according to color. For example, you could string beads in a red, blue, red, blue, red, blue pattern. Once you begin the pattern, ask your child to extend it.

When your child feels comfortable creating AB patterns, demonstrate other types of patterns, such as ABB or AABB or ABC. It is not necessary to use colored objects to create patterns. Consider using knives, forks, and spoons from the kitchen.

Extending the activity

When your child feels comfortable creating patterns with colors, explore creating patterns with numbers. For example, write a sequence of numbers that follows a pattern, such as 2, 4, 6, 8 . . . or 3, 6, 9, 12 . . . . Ask your child what number comes next. Have him or her explain what the pattern is. (*Counting by twos or threes*)

What your child is practicing

Patterns are an essential part of mathematics. When children are first learning patterning, it is easier for them to extend patterns that you have started than to create them on their own. Each time you introduce a new pattern (AABBCC, ABCDABCD, and so on), begin by starting the pattern and then have your child extend it. Do this several times with each pattern before asking him or her to create a pattern. Learning to recognize and create patterns builds a strong mathematical foundation.

Sorting the Laundry

Targeted skill

Children are expected to sort objects according to their attributes and describe how those groups are formed.

Materials

♦ a basket of clean (or dirty) clothes

What to do

At laundry time, ask your child to "be a detective" and help you solve the problem of sorting the laundry into different groups.

Tell him or her what groups you want the clothes to be divided into, such as light-colored clothes and dark-colored clothes; dad's socks and children's socks; big brother's clothes and little brother's clothes.

Then indicate an area where the different groups should be placed, and give your child the first piece of clothing. As your child correctly sorts the clothes, encourage him or her to talk about why each object belongs in that particular group. For example, he or she might say, "This sock is small so I know that it belongs in the child pile, not the grown-up pile."

Sorting the Laundry (continued)

Extending the activity

✤ The ways to sort the laundry are limited only by your imagination. Your child can sort by color, the clothing's use, size, shape, and so on.

✤ Your child can also create patterns with the laundry, using large and small socks to make patterns (ABAB, AAB, AABB, and so on).

✤ Taking the piles of sorted laundry to the correct place also helps your child associate an object with its use, such as returning bath towels to the bathroom and dish towels to the kitchen.

✤ Your child could extend the sorting activity into a matching activity. For example, after sorting socks into "children" and "grown-up" piles, he or she could then match the single socks into pairs.

✤ Laundry time offers lots of opportunities for mathematical learning. For example, calling attention to the way you measure the detergent makes your child aware of how measurement is used in daily activities. Counting the number of shirts or socks offers a chance for learning counting and comparing quantities.

> ### What your child is practicing
>
> By sorting the laundry, your child is practicing grouping objects by their attributes. He or she has to remember the distinguishing qualities of each group and make decisions accordingly to place the objects in the correct group.

Coupon Sort

Targeted skill

Young children are expected to match, sort, and compare numbers as well as sort objects by different categories (for example, by their use).

Materials

- Coupon Sorting Mat
- coupon inserts from Sunday newspapers
- scissors
- index cards
- glue
- envelopes

What to do

Coupon Sort is a simple game to create, and it can be used in lots of different ways that support mathematical learning as well as letter naming and phonological awareness.

The first thing you and your child should do is cut out coupons. (Using scissors to cut straight lines helps strengthen your child's fine-motor skills, which in turn helps his or her handwriting.) After cutting out the coupons, glue each one onto an index card.

At first, ask your child to put together coupons that have the same number on them. This is simply a matter of matching. Once he or she can do this, you can introduce a different way to sort coupons: by the place in your house you would put the item. Using the sorting mat, have your child examine each coupon and decide if the associated item should be put into the "kitchen cabinet," the "refrigerator," or the "bathroom."

After you have made a collection of coupon cards, you can begin to use the collection for different math skills.

Coupon Sort *(continued)*

Extending the activity

When your child becomes accomplished with double-digit numbers, have him or her place the coupons in numerical order. At first, limit the collection to only two coupon values, for example, 10 and 25 cents off. Then have your child sort these, putting the 10-cents-off coupons on the left and the 25-cents-off coupons on the right, talking about smaller and larger numbers. When this seems easy for your child, add another number, then another, and another, as your child's ability to order numbers increases.

What your child is practicing

Your child needs lots of experiences with numbers in order to understand how they relate to one another. The Coupon Sort activity provides this and connects numbers to the real world.

Coupon Sorting Mat

Kitchen Cabinet

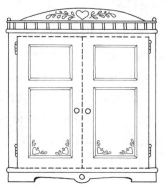

Refrigerator

Bathroom

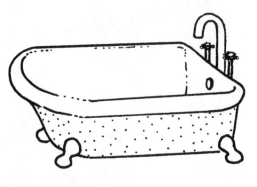

Guess My Rule

Targeted skill

Young children are expected to see similarities and differences between objects and group them accordingly. They are also learning to use reason and logically support their thinking, that is, use and apply problem-solving strategies.

Materials

- small objects such as colored blocks or buttons
- envelopes

What to do

Place several small objects in the playing area. Think of a way that similar objects might be grouped and begin to select the objects that fit that rule, saying, "This object fits my rule. Can you guess my rule?" Keep selecting objects that fit the rule until your child can identify the rule.

For example, if your rule is "buttons with two holes," first select a large, flat button with two holes and a small, square button with two holes from the group. Say, "These buttons fit my rule. Can you guess my rule?" After that, select more buttons that fit the rule. You can also identify objects that do not fit the rule. Give your child support as he or she discovers the rule.

Extending the activity

- As your child gets better at this activity, increase the difficulty of the rule. For example, make the rule something that is not obvious. Often children look for rules that apply to colors or shapes first, so select rules that involve other attributes.

- This activity can be done anywhere. Create groups using various rules, such as girls with long hair, boys wearing shorts, cars with the windows rolled down, men wearing hats.

- Ask your child to help you list all the attributes of a particular object. Then use one of those attributes as your rule.

What your child is practicing

With opportunities to explain his or her thinking and logically work through a problem until he or she finds a solution, your child is practicing lifelong mathematical skills.

Act It Out

Targeted skill

Young children are expected to model and create addition and subtraction problems in real situations with concrete objects.

Materials

♦ stuffed animals, dolls, cars, or other small toys

What to do

Gather a small assortment of toys and ask your child to use them to represent mathematical problems. For example, you might say, "Two bears were sitting on a log. Another bear came by to join them on the log. How many bears are sitting on the log?" Use stuffed bears to "act out" the story and help your child count the bears to get the correct answer.

Extending the activity

✤ Be sure to balance addition and subtraction problems. Since "adding more" is often easier for young children to understand, adults tend to offer those kinds of story problems more often. "Taking away" is a bit harder to understand, so be sure to include such problems as well.

✤ Enlist the help of family members to act out story problems. Actually having people enter (or leave) a space provides your child with another kind of visual for the story problems.

✤ Acting out stories that relate to family activities can keep your child's attention focused for longer periods of time. For example, use boxes or cans of food to act out problems such as "Mary has three cans of vegetables. The family eats one can. How many cans are left?"

Act It Out (continued)

More questions to ask

✤ Ask your child "what if" questions. For example, after your child has acted out a particular situation, ask him or her, "What if there had been two more?" This extends your child's learning and challenges him or her to look at familiar things in a different way.

✤ Using mathematical language in such situations helps your child understand mathematical terms. Simply saying, "Wow, when two cars joined that one car, you had *more* cars than you started with," helps your child associate the meaning of *more* with an increasing number. Math terms such as *more/fewer, greater/less, larger/smaller* are often confusing for young children. Using them over and over can help your child understand their meanings.

What your child is practicing

Your child is using his or her toys to accurately represent numbers and the way they are combined and separated. Since this is often a hard concept for young children to grasp, it is helpful to offer many different ways of representing a math problem. Further, physically acting out a problem helps make those abstract ideas clearer.

Guess and Check

Targeted skill

Young children are expected to reason and support their thinking while using mathematical language. They are also expected to use a problem-solving model that incorporates understanding the problem, making a plan to solve it, carrying out the plan, and evaluating the solution for reasonableness.

Materials

- small objects such as blocks or buttons
- small cloth to cover the blocks (wash cloth or small towel works well)

What to do

In Guess and Check, your child makes a reasonable prediction about an answer and then checks to confirm the prediction. This process helps young children who are used to making guesses without any reasoning behind them begin to assess the reasonableness of their guesses.

Place the objects in the center of the playing area. Ask your child to combine a given number of objects. For example, say, "Put two blue blocks and one red block in the center of the table." Cover the blocks with a small cloth. Ask, "How many blocks are in the center?" Ask your child to support his or her answer: "Why do you think that three is the answer?" Expect your child to give a logical explanation such as, "I think there are three because I had two and then got one more. Three is one more than two." Then remove the cloth and ask your child to "check" by counting the blocks. Ask, "Was your prediction reasonable?" to help your child assess his or her original prediction.

Guess and Check *(continued)*

Extending the activity

✤ As your child's ability increases, make the math problems more and more difficult.

✤ Use a variety of objects to play this game. Using sticks, marbles, pinecones, and other items adds variety to the same activity.

More questions to ask

Asking "Is it reasonable?" is appropriate in many situations. As mathematical language becomes an everyday part of your child's vocabulary, he or she will have a better understanding of various mathematical terms.

What your child is practicing

Learning to make reasonable estimates is hard for young children. They are not used to taking several variables into account before they make a decision. Learning to do so carries over from math situations into the realm of language arts as well.

What Comes in Twos and Threes?

Targeted skill

Young children are expected to improve their number sense as they learn that numbers have a relationship to groups of objects, for example, that objects can come in pairs.

Materials

♦ collection of things that come in twos (shoes, socks, eyes, hands, ears, arms, legs, sleeves in a jacket, legs in pants, bicycle tires)

♦ collection of things that come in threes (tricycle tires, sides of a triangle, three little pigs, three bears)

What to do

To begin playing, show your child just one "thing" that comes in twos, and then challenge him or her to go through the house looking for other things that come in twos. For example, you might discuss how one sock matched with another sock makes a pair, or two socks. Challenge him or her to notice other twos (or pairs of objects).

On another day, show your child just one "thing" that comes in threes, and then challenge him or her to go through the house looking for other things that come in threes. It helps in early games of What Comes in Twos and Threes? to put sets of twos and threes in plain sight around the house. For example, you might place a knife, fork, and spoon in clear view on the kitchen cabinet or move the tricycle to a prominent place in the garage.

It is not enough for young children to see the numeral 2 and be able to recognize it. Children need to see many sets of twos, so that over time, they begin to develop number sense about the numeral 2. They also need to understand the relationship among numbers—that three is more than two, that two is more than one.

What your child is practicing

Looking for mathematical concepts in his or her environment helps your child truly understand that numbers are more than just a "school thing."

Extending the activity

While it will be more difficult to locate things that come in larger numbers, challenge the whole family to look for such things. For example, car tires, dog legs, and sides of squares come in fours; fingers, toes, and sides of a pentagon come in fives.

Just-Right Homework Activities for PreK–K © 2009 by Diffily & Sassman, Scholastic Teaching Resources

Finding Shapes in the House

Targeted skill

Young children are expected to recognize shapes in real-life objects and describe, identify, and compare circles, triangles, and rectangles, including squares.

What to do

While this activity involves "just looking" around the house, it is looking with a purpose. First, be sure that your child knows the attributes of the shape that he or she is looking for. For example, you might draw a shape on a piece of paper (or have your child draw or copy your example). Then describe the lines that make up that shape. You might say, "This is a triangle. See how three lines make a shape with three sides. We can turn this shape any direction and it still makes a triangle."

Then, challenge your child to find triangular shapes in your house. The shape might be found in a lamp's design, a pattern in the couch's fabric, or a picture on the wall.

Begin with the shapes that are most common in your home, probably rectangles (doors, windows, light switches, picture frames), then circles (doorknobs, plates, flowerpots), then triangles.

Extending the activity

✤ Once your child understands these basic shapes, introduce him or her to other shapes, such as the pentagon or octagon.

Finding Shapes in the House *(continued)*

❖ Make a shape book with your child. Staple together several pages and label each page with the name of a shape. Walk around your house with your child, and as he or she points out a shape, encourage him or her to draw that shape on the appropriate page.

❖ Count how many examples of a single shape you can find in your house. For example, begin in the kitchen and count how many rectangles you find there. Then move to the bedroom and count the rectangles there. Compare these two numbers using such words as *most* and *fewest*, *greater* and *lesser*.

❖ Many of your child's toys incorporate these shapes. Be sure to point out to your child the connection between these shapes. For example, point out that the rectangles in the windows of her dollhouse and the rectangle formed by the top of the coffee table each have two long sides and two short sides.

❖ This activity can be done anywhere—in the garage, at the park, in the backyard. Make finding shapes an activity to use when waiting in the doctor's office or for the bus.

❖ Play with shapes! Form shapes with your body, for example, hold your arms together in a circle or bend your knees to form a diamond.

❖ Trace familiar shapes using common household items such as jar lids, cookie cutters, medium-sized puzzle pieces, or blocks. Be sure to talk about the characteristics of the shape as your child is tracing.

More questions to ask

Discuss with your child the differences between shapes. Ask how many more (or fewer) sides does a particular shape have than another. Ask what makes one shape different from another.

What your child is practicing

Understanding that shapes are used all around us is a complicated concept for young children. This activity helps your child learn to look closely at objects and make critical evaluations of them. That is, you are teaching your child to look and evaluate before making a decision. Our grandmothers called that "looking before you leap."

Finding Shapes in the Neighborhood

Targeted skill

Young children are expected to recognize shapes in real-life objects and describe, identify, and compare circles, triangles, and rectangles, including squares.

What to do

As you are walking down the street or sitting on the porch, draw your child's attention to geometric shapes that you observe. This activity can be done like the traditional I Spy game, with you saying, "I spy a large rectangle," and your child answering, "Is it the neighbor's front door?"

Extending the activity

✤ You can also "find" more than one shape at a time, such as saying, "I spy five rectangles" to accommodate the windows of the neighbor's house.

✤ Shapes can also be found in neighborhood signs. Traffic signs as well as billboards often contain recognizable shapes. As you walk in the neighborhood, call your child's attention to the various signs.

✤ Look for shapes in unusual places—the wheels of a bike or car, the shape of a flower, the shape of manicured shrubbery.

✤ Encourage your child to record all the different shapes he or she observes. Keeping an Observation Journal can be an ongoing activity for you and your child. Remind your child to take the journal as you go on errands and to regularly add entries to it.

✤ This activity can also be done with three-dimensional shapes, such as an ice-cream cone for a cone or a trash can for a cylinder.

What your child is practicing

Seeing shapes in unexpected places helps your child learn to make close observations and relate things he or she observes to things that he or she knows. Making those connections is important for young children.

Shapes Go Fish

Targeted skill

Young children are expected to learn the names of basic shapes and their distinguishing characteristics.

Materials

♦ index cards

♦ markers

What to do

Create a set of 24 playing cards out of index cards. Make eight cards with a triangle, eight with a square, and eight with a circle. If more than two or three people are playing, you need to make more cards to allow enough matches for everyone. Shapes Go Fish is played like any other game of Go Fish.

To play:

1. Shuffle the cards and deal four cards to each player. Stack the remaining cards facedown between the players. Turn one card faceup.

2. The goal of the game is to collect a set of four of the same shape.

3. The first player selects a shape in his hand and asks one player if he or she has that particular shape. If the player does, he or she must give it to the player who asked for it.

4. Player 1 can continue asking other players for specific cards, until one of the players does not hold the requested card. This player responds, "Go fish." Then Player 1 takes the card on top of the remainder pile and discards one card. Player 2 takes a turn.

5. The first player to get four cards with the same shape wins.

Shape Go Fish *(continued)*

When your child is able to consistently recognize the three primary shapes—circle, square, and triangle—add other shapes, one at a time (rectangle, diamond, trapezoid, pentagon, hexagon, octagon, semicircle, rhombus).

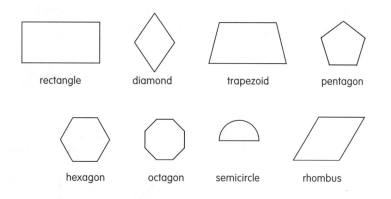

rectangle diamond trapezoid pentagon

hexagon octagon semicircle rhombus

If your family is used to playing Go Fish with particular rules, you may follow those rules or customs when playing Shapes Go Fish. The intent is to learn the names of the shapes, not cause controversy over the rules.

Extending the activity

Go on a scavenger hunt around the house or in the neighborhood to look for shapes in the environment. For example, a door is a rectangle, the light-switch plate (for two switches) is a square, coins are circles, and paper money is a rectangle. However, you want to stress that the *surface* of the desk is a rectangle, the *surface* of the door is a rectangle, the *surface* of the clock is a circle, and so on. You do not want your child to continue thinking that a ball is a circle and a block is a rectangle. (A ball is a sphere and a block is a rectangular prism.)

What your child is practicing

Learning to identify shapes begins the process of understanding geometry. Your child needs many different experiences with seeing and naming shapes in simple drawings and within his or her environment before he or she learns and understands them.

Hexagons and Triangles

Targeted skill

Young children are expected to learn one-to-one correspondence between the dots on the die and the number of game pieces to be put on the board and how to exchange items of like value, such as six triangles for one hexagon.

Materials

♦ game board   ♦ die

What to do

This is a simple game. Before playing, cut out the triangle and hexagon shapes from the reproducible page. Put the game board and game pieces in the playing area.

To play:

1. Player 1 rolls the die and counts the number of dots. Then he or she counts out that number of triangle game pieces and places them on a hexagon on the game board.

2. Players take turns rolling the die and collecting triangle game pieces. When a player has covered an entire hexagon, he or she can choose to exchange the six triangles for one hexagon shape. Then the player rolls the die again to collect more triangles to cover the other hexagons on the game board.

3. Play continues until all the shapes are covered with hexagons.

Extending the activity

As children get comfortable counting die dots up to six, change the game a bit. Ask players to roll two dice, so that the dots on the dice have to be added together.

What your child is practicing

Your child is developing the mathematical concept of regrouping and exchange. Very soon, your child will need to understand that a group of 10 ones is the same as 1 ten. Later, your child will learn that two nickels are the same as one dime, four quarters are the same as one dollar, and five dimes and two quarters are the same as one dollar. Hexagons and Triangles introduces your child to this concept.

Hexagons and Triangles
Game Board

Hexagons and Triangles
Game Pieces

Teacher: Make two copies of this page for each player.

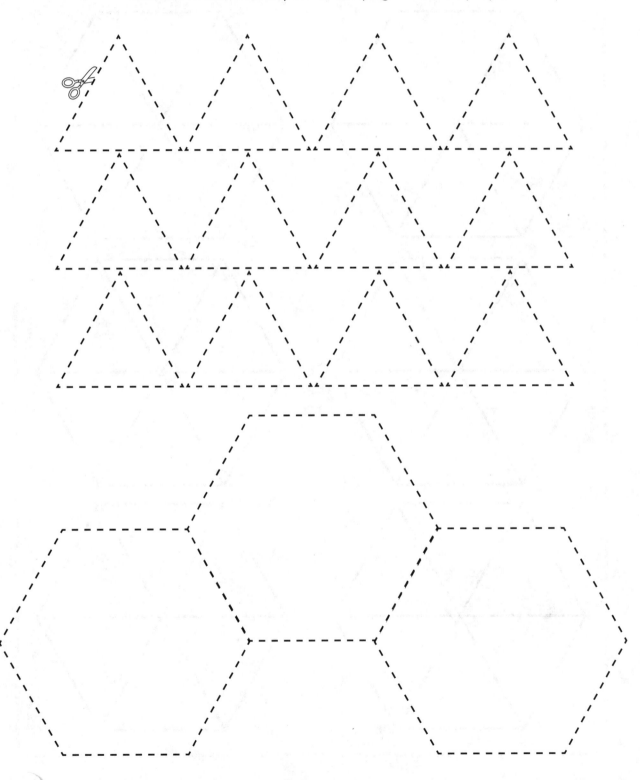

Small, Medium, and Large

Targeted skill

Young children are expected to sort items by size. Judgment and decision-making are also called for.

Materials

♦ objects that come in small, medium, and large sizes (for example, washcloth, hand towel, and bath towel; salad fork, dinner fork, and serving fork; dime, nickel, and quarter; a golf ball, a softball, and a soccer ball)

♦ 2 sheets of 8 ½-by-11-inch paper

What to do

To make the sorting mats for this game, simply use a large piece of paper for the large mat (an 8 ½-by-11-inch sheet of paper). Then cut another sheet in half for the medium mat (8 ½-by-5 ½ inches), and cut the other half in half again for the small mat (5 ½-by-4 ¼ inches).

At first, provide several of the objects listed above and encourage your child to put the small object on the small sorting mat, the medium object on the medium sorting mat, and the large object on the large sorting mat. This task seems quite easy from an adult perspective, but understanding and sorting by relative size is an early math concept that young children need to practice before they master.

After your child has done this several times, challenge him or her to go around the house and look for things that come in different sizes (pieces of clothing from family members—socks, shoes, shirts, slacks, and so on).

Extending the activity

Once your child seems to grasp the ability to identify small, medium, and large objects, challenge him or her to draw small, medium, and large things.

What your child is practicing

In this activity your child is sorting objects by their size. Children seem to naturally sort things by color, shape, and size. Watch your child with a handful of candy and he or she will often separate the candy into the different colors. Many young children sort their cars by color and sort their blocks by their shapes. You can use this tendency to sort things to make learning early math skills a natural part of your child's life.

Shorter, Longer

Targeted skill

Young children are expected to learn the length of two objects and identify the one that is shorter and the one that is longer.

Materials

♦ almost anything in the house, but start with familiar objects whose lengths can be easily compared, such as spoon to knife, pencil to pen, or toothpick to spatula

What to do

This activity consists of comparing two objects and using the correct mathematical terms—*shorter* or *longer*. You can do this activity at the dinner table using flatware or have your child sort through the family's junk drawer to find objects: paper clips, pencils, pens, envelopes, index cards, and so on.

Simply line up two objects and model for your child. You might say, "This one is shorter and this one is longer," as you point to each object in turn. Then ask your child to choose two objects and make the same judgment. Be sure your child uses the correct mathematical terms of *shorter* and *longer*.

Extending the activity

✤ When your child can consistently identify the shorter and longer object (and use the correct term for each), add another object, so that your child has to order the three items by length. Arrange the objects so that they all have the same starting point. For example, place the ends of each object along the edge of the table. Sometimes young children have difficulty aligning the ends of objects. Your child needs many experiences before he or she realizes that this is an important part of measurement.

✤ When your child can order four or five objects, begin introducing other terms used to compare objects: *taller* and *shorter*, *narrower* and *wider*.

What your child is practicing

These activities are the beginning steps of understanding measurement. Your child must grasp this concept before he or she begins to use a ruler to determine a standard measure, such as inches or feet.

Spoon Measurement

Targeted skill

Young children are expected to compare and order two or three concrete objects according to volume, determining which one holds more or less. They are also measuring according to volume rather than the more common measurement of length.

Materials

- 3 or 4 small, clear containers (clear plastic cups or containers that hold leftover food work well, as long as they're all the same size)
- spoons (large measuring spoons or scoops work well)
- container of water
- towels

What to do

This activity can be done outside, on the kitchen floor, or on the countertop—anywhere that spills can be easily cleaned up. Placing a towel under the work surface helps collect drips and spills. Keeping another towel nearby is a good idea also.

Place the three containers on the surface. Ask your child to place a given number of spoonfuls of water into the first container. Ask him or her to do the same for the other containers, varying the amount of water in each one.

Then ask your child to place the containers in order from least amount of water to greatest. Discuss his or her thinking. Talk about looking at the level of water in the container. Help your child realize the relationship between the number of spoonfuls of water put in the container with the volume of the water.

Repeat the activity with a larger spoon, then with a smaller spoon. Continue to use the mathematical terms of *more*, *less*, *greater than*, and *less than*.

Spoon Measurement *(continued)*

Extending the activity

❖ Vary the size of the containers. For example, gather three large containers and three small containers. Compare how the water level differs, depending on the size of the container.

❖ Use bath time as an opportunity for this activity, placing the containers on the side of the tub.

❖ If your child has difficulty seeing the water level, use a few drops of food coloring to tint the water.

❖ Encourage your child to use the markings on a measuring cup to describe his or her activities. If the cup has too many marks and is confusing, use a permanent marker to mark ¼-, ½-, and ¾-full positions on a plain container.

What your child is practicing

Young children do not get much practice with measuring liquids or determining volume. Using mathematical terms, like *more* or *less*, while doing these activities helps your child's understanding.

Paper-Clip Measurement

Targeted skill

Young children are expected to order objects according to length and identify objects that are about the same length as, or of a lesser or greater length than, a given object.

Materials

◆ several paper clips

◆ several small objects to measure (various lengths of pencils, pieces of yarn, screws, nails)

What to do

This activity involves using nonstandard measurement to determine the length of an object. Ask your child to place the paper clips beside the object, placing the end of the first one at the end of the object and lining them up end to end. Then ask him or her to count them and say how long the object is in paper clips; for example, "The pencil is seven paper clips long." If the object is longer (or shorter) than the paper clips, use the term *about* to round up (or down) to the closest length.

Extending the activity

✤ Your child can use the paper clips to measure other objects in the house. Help him or her measure the length of the place mat, fork, and knife at dinner, tools in the garage, and the height of toys.

✤ Ask your child to compare and describe the length of two (or more) objects, using such language as, "The screwdriver is one paper clip longer than the pliers." Help your child use mathematical terms such as *longer than*, *shorter than*, *greater than*, and *less than*.

✤ As your child becomes accustomed to measuring with paper clips, have him or her measure with other smaller or larger objects such as pennies, buttons, toothpicks, or blocks. Help your child understand that the length of an object might be described as four toothpicks long or as seven buttons long. Help him or her understand that the length of an object does not change but the way it is described does change according to the unit of measurement.

What your child is practicing

Assigning a number to the length of an object can be confusing for young children. Practicing and talking about the concept helps your child understand it.

Favorite Foods

Targeted skill

Young children are expected to learn how to collect data and create charts to show the data. They are also learning to make assumptions from the data, such as "since more people in our family drink water than drink soda, our family needs to buy more water than soda."

Materials

- writing paper
- pencil, pen, crayon, or felt-tip marker

What to do

This is a good activity to do at dinnertime. Ask your child to choose two foods (for example, hamburgers and pizza). They do not have to be ones that are served for that meal. They might be family favorites or your child's favorites. Help your child divide a piece of paper in half, writing "hamburgers" on one side and "pizza" on the other (or ask your child to draw a picture of each food). Have your child ask each person in the family to indicate which of the two foods he or she prefers and mark each person's vote.

Help your child associate the number of tally marks with the number of people he or she asked. Have him or her decide which number is larger.

Extending the activity

- This way of collecting data can be repeated with any number of things, such as favorite foods, favorite colors, or favorite television programs. And you should not limit your child to surveying just the immediate family. Ask him or her to do this activity with extended family members and/or family friends.

- Find ways to encourage your child to apply this skill in ways to help the family. For example, at a family gathering, your child might survey the group to see how many people want water, tea, or soda to drink. Any time that your child can use the skill he or she is learning for a real-world reason, he or she will be more eager to accomplish the task.

What your child is practicing

Probability and statistics may be a sophisticated form of mathematics, but it starts with simply collecting and recording data.

Life Timeline

Targeted skill

Mathematicians collect and record data, that is, they gather and write down information, to help them understand a problem. Young children are learning to collect and record data about their lives in this activity. Further, they are practicing probability and statistics as they construct a simple graph or timeline and use the information from that graph to answer questions.

Materials

◆ paper

◆ pencil

◆ records from your child's early years, such as picture albums or a baby book

What to do

Divide a piece of paper into sections, one for each year of your child's life. Label (or help your child label) each section with your child's age during that year.

Beginning with the current year, write (or draw or help your child write or draw) a few events to represent that year's activities. Continue to add activities for each year of your child's life. Record milestones such as first steps, first word, and first vacation.

Extending the activity

✤ This activity can be as simple or complex as you and your child want. Record only a few events for each year at first, then add more as your child's interest indicates. Add mementos that you may have.

✤ Add the year to the labels above each year of your child's life. Discuss that years are numbered in order, asking what year would come after (or before) a given year.

Life Timeline *(continued)*

❖ Make this timeline in either a horizontal or vertical format (or both). Young children need to learn that the same information can be displayed in different ways.

❖ Share this activity with interested family members, such as grandparents. This gives your child another opportunity to describe the events of his or her life.

❖ Help your child glue photographs representative of each year's activities to the timeline. Vacations, family reunions, birth of brothers or sisters, and holiday celebrations are all good choices. Be sure to include things that are special to your family, such as hobbies or customs.

❖ Be sure to celebrate your child's accomplishments for each year. Encourage your child to realize that he or she worked hard to master a particular skill that he or she now take for granted. Tell fun or encouraging stories about how he or she worked hard and made mistakes before mastering a skill.

❖ Turn this activity into a story time. When describing an event to your child, make sure to describe how you felt, other people's responses, the weather, and any smells or special sounds. Including all these things will help him or her understand how these qualities make stories more interesting.

What your child is practicing

Once young children master a skill, they believe that they have *always* possessed it. Making a timeline of your child's life helps him or her understand change over time, his or her own development, how to organize information, and how to get information from a chart or graph.

My Day

Targeted skill

It can be difficult for young children to understand the concept of the passage of time. Noticing that events happen "first, second, and third" is the first step to mastering the concept.

Materials

◆ 3 pieces of paper of the same size

◆ crayons

What to do

On the first piece of paper, ask your child to draw pictures of the foods he or she ate at breakfast. On the next piece, draw foods from lunch, and on the third, foods from dinner. Turn the papers facedown and mix them up. Ask your child to select each one and describe it. He or she might say, "This picture shows what I ate for breakfast." Then ask your child to arrange the pictures in order. Encourage him or her to use the words *first*, *second*, and *third* as he or she arranges the pictures.

Or help your child sketch several events that occurred during a particular day. They do not have to be special events, just the daily routine of folding clothes, watching cartoons, or picking up groceries is okay. Then place these events in the order in which they occurred. Using the terms *first*, *second*, *third*, and so on is important.

Extending the activity

❖ Work with your child to draw pictures that represent individual years in his or her life. For example, for the first year the drawing could have a sketch of a baby, a bottle, and a favorite toy. For the second year, it could have a sketch of a particular achievement or family event. Then help your child arrange these drawings in order to represent his or her life. Be sure to encourage your child to use the mathematical terms of *first*, *second*, *third*, *fourth*, and so on.

❖ During a long weekend or family vacation, help your child draw a sketch of each day's events. Then help him or her arrange them in order. Staple the pages together (include a title page and end page) to make a journal of the event.

What your child is practicing

Using the terms *first, second, third, fourth*, and so on helps your child understand the ordinal numbers.

Introduction to Reading and Writing Homework

Language and literacy homework is often just "read aloud for 20 minutes." While we are advocates for students reading each and every day, there is so much more to learn than just basic "word calling," especially with pre-kindergarten and kindergarten students. These activities are designed to provide families with specific ways to enrich their child's language and literacy, while going beyond reading for a certain number of minutes.

These activities address such skills as vocabulary development, letter recognition, decoding, comprehension, and writing. Parents often need help in understanding how to integrate these skills into their day-to-day family life. For example, many parents do not think of asking their child to look at or identify the letters on their favorite fast-food restaurant's sign or logo. While we, as teachers, see this as a natural progression, the families are more concerned with making sure everyone eats, that the children have time to play on the playground, and so on. The activities in this section address how to make learning a part of the family routine.

These literacy activities seek to offer busy families ways to integrate the learning into daily family life. Additionally, the activities are designed to be enjoyable for the family to do together, and they are designed to include younger and older siblings, grandparents, aunts, uncles, and any other family members who may be present.

Kitchen Study

Targeted skill

Young children are expected to connect experiences and ideas with those of others through speaking and listening.

Materials

♦ kitchen items, such as stove, pots and pans, and cooking utensils

What to do

Using objects commonly found in the kitchen to engage your child in conversation extends and enriches his or her vocabulary and use of oral language.

You might begin by pulling out all the bowls in the kitchen and placing them on the floor. Ask your child to stack the bowls so they will fit in the cabinet (or arrange them in some other fashion). Engage your child in conversation about the bowls. Say things such as, "Tell me about that bowl," encouraging him or her to use words to describe the bowl's size, shape, color, and so on.

Extending the activity

❖ Encourage your child to compare two similar objects, using words to describe how the two objects are alike and different.

❖ This activity can be done with lots of common household objects, such as things found in the bathroom, bedroom, or garage. Be sure to supervise the selection of objects to keep your child safe.

❖ Encourage your child to use unfamiliar words. For example, if *oval* is a new word, encourage him or her to find other oval objects. Young children need many experiences with a word before they learn its meaning and begin to use it on their own.

What your child is practicing

Children need practice in many activities to help develop their oral language skills. Your child is learning to express himself or herself in complete thoughts and link these thoughts together to make conversations. These oral language skills are basic to learning to read and write.

Labeling a Room

Targeted skill

Young children must learn to connect an initial consonant sound with the letter that represents it.

Materials

- ◆ index cards
- ◆ felt-tip markers or pencils
- ◆ tape

What to do

This is a quick and easy way to take your child's interest in language and make it a learning activity. When your child expresses interest in beginning sounds, make labels of common objects in your home. In the beginning, write only the letter that makes the first sound of the object. Label the door as "D," the sofa as "S," and so on. As your child's knowledge grows, begin to label objects with the whole word— label the stove as "stove" and the chair as "chair."

Remember to keep this simple and begin by labeling only a few things at a time. Begin with signs that incorporate only one letter—"D" for door, "S" for sofa, and so on.

Extending the activity

✤ At the simplest level, begin by wearing a label with an "M" for mom or "D" for dad. Remind your child of the letters and the sound that they make. Periodically, ask your child to name the letter as you point to the sign. Remember that young children need many opportunities to practice a skill before they learn it.

✤ Once children get used to seeing the same signs day after day, they do not notice them anymore. After your child's interest wanes, replace the signs with new ones.

✤ Be sure to include your child in the preparation of the signs. Carefully form the letters, talking through each stroke, and then give the signs to your child to place on the objects.

What your child is practicing

Young children have learned that speaking specific words gets them what they want. The youngest children learn that saying "wa-wa" gets them a drink. By labeling objects in your house, you are helping your child take the next step of associating a letter's form with a sound. Making the connection that reading is talking written down is critical to helping children understand the basics of reading.

What Is This Color?

Targeted skill

Young children are expected to learn to associate an object's name with its attributes, such as color and shape.

Materials

♦ markers or crayons

♦ anything in the house that is an easy-to-identify color

What to do

When children are first learning to name colors, begin with only one. For example, show your child a red crayon and ask, "What is this color?" Whether he or she says, "red" or another color, respond with "Red. This is a red crayon. Let's find something else that is red." Then look through the house for other things that are red. You might have red shirts or socks in the bedroom or red flowers in the yard. Find as many red things as you can, each time using a full sentence to name the color and the object, such as "This is a red flower," and have your child repeat the sentence after you.

You can do this little game with any color. Over time, the repetition of finding colored items and naming their color will help your child remember what each color is called.

Extending the activity

After playing this game for a few days, review color names by showing your child crayons or markers and have him or her identify color names that you have practiced recently.

What your child is practicing

As your child learns to name the color of objects, he or she is learning one type of adjective. Using adjectives expands a child's vocabulary by describing things. Instead of "ball," encourage your child to begin to use expanded language, such as "red ball." Identifying colors of objects is also the first way that children usually begin categorizing objects. The skill of sorting is an important basic math skill for young children to master.

Concepts of Print

Targeted skill

Young children are expected to understand concepts of print, which connect reading with print awareness. Understanding them is fundamental to beginning to learn to read.

Materials

♦ a book, magazine, or other printed material (simple, familiar books are best)

What to do

Helping your child understand concepts of print is an ongoing activity. Every time you sit down with your child to read, remind him or her of one of the following concepts. Suggest them in informal situations, praise your child when he or she uses a correct term, and consistently use the correct terms yourself—in general, take advantage of every opportunity to acquaint your child with reading.

Hand your child a book with the cover facing away from him or her. Ask how he or she knew to turn the book to the front. Say, "Yes, the *cover* of a book shows us the front."

Point out the ways in which the title page and the cover are similar. Show your child that the title page sometimes includes more information, such as the publisher, the city where the book was published, and the copyright.

Begin reading by moving your finger under the words on the page. When your reach the end of the page, ask, "Where do I go next?" As your child indicates the next page to the right, say, "Yes, when we read we start on the *left* and go to the *right*. That's what readers do."

Call your child's attention to the illustration on a page. Discuss with him or her how features of the picture match the words on the page. You might isolate a particular word (using your fingers to block out the other words). Say, "Wow! You found a dog on the page and this word says *dog*. That matches!"

Use the terms *author* and *illustrator* to help your child understand who writes the words and draws the pictures.

Concepts of Print (continued)

Extending the activity

❖ Compare two books by the same author and illustrator. Discuss that the illustrator usually draws in a similar style or that the author usually writes about similar characters.

❖ Spread out several books in front of your child. Ask him or her to find the same element in each book. Point out that most books have the same elements, but they may not look the same from book to book.

❖ Sometimes young children are intrigued by the copyright date of a book. They like to compare the age of the book with their age. You could place several books by the same author or illustrator in chronological order and look to see how that author's or illustrator's style has changed over time.

More questions to ask

As your child understands the cover, the way words move from left to right on the page, the difference between the illustration and words, and so on, begin to introduce more sophisticated concepts. Ask your child to slide the pointer finger of each hand along to indicate one word or one letter. Point to a period and ask what it is used for, explaining if your child doesn't know or understand. Continue with an exclamation point, question mark, and comma.

What your child is practicing

"Concepts of print" is a complicated way of saying that young children understand that the writing on a page represents spoken words and that it has meaning. It also refers to children's understanding of such writing conventions as moving left to right across the page, separating words with spaces, distinguishing between one letter and a whole word, knowing the difference between capital and lowercase letters, and recognizing that readers use capital letters and punctuation to help with the meaning. Further, it also includes teaching children the names and purposes for the parts of a book, such as the cover, title page, and table of contents.

Picture Walks

Targeted skill

Young children are expected to develop an understanding of the structure of stories—that they have a beginning, middle, and end—as well as learn to recognize the relationship between the text and illustrations.

Materials

◆ a children's book with strong illustrations

What to do

Before opening the book, show your child the cover and read the title. Ask him or her to predict what the story will be about, based only on what he or she can see. Slowly flip through the book, page by page, without reading a single word. Ask questions about each picture, and try to elicit responses that require your child to make inferences based upon the images, and not the words, on each page.

Starting with the five Ws (who, what, when, where, why) and one H (how), you can ask plenty of questions to engage your child's imagination and encourage his or her active participation.

Ask questions such as, "*What* is going on here?" "*Who* is this?" "*Why* does the character look so excited?" "*When* is this story taking place?" "*Where* did the character just come from?" "*How* do you think the story is going to end?"

This way, you are leading your child in telling the story of the book just by paying close attention to the illustrations.

Extending the activity

After doing several picture walks together, encourage your child to tell the story of a picture book independently.

What your child is practicing

When your child answers questions about the pictures in a story, he or she practices paying close attention to illustrations and putting his or her thoughts into words. With a bit of encouragement, this is also a time when your child practices using complete sentences to answer questions. When your child reaches the stage at which he or she can do a picture walk on his or her own, your child is practicing the way stories "sound."

Dialogic Reading

Targeted skill

The questions during Dialogic Reading strengthen young children's listening comprehension, and strong listening comprehension leads to strong reading comprehension.

Materials

♦ any children's book

What to do

Dialogic reading is a fancy way of saying, "Read a book to your child and ask questions before, during, and after reading it." While it is always a good idea to read aloud to your child, this experience becomes more educational when your child is encouraged to think about the story by answering the questions who, what, when, where, why, and how. This type of questioning engages your child as an active participant in the read-aloud. In thinking of questions about storybooks, sometimes it helps to use the acronym CROWD:

Completion prompts – You leave a blank at the end of a sentence and get your child to fill it in. These are typically used in books with rhyme or books with repetitive phrases. For example, you might read, "I think I'd be a glossy cat. A little plump but not too ____," letting your child fill in the blank with the word *fat*. Completion prompts provide children with information about the structure of language that is critical to later reading.

Recall prompts – These are questions about what happened in a book. Recall prompts work for nearly everything except alphabet books. For example, you might say, "Can you tell me what happened to the little blue engine in this story?" Recall prompts help children understand a story's plot and describe the sequence of events.

Open-ended prompts – These prompts focus on the pictures in books. They work best for books that have detailed illustrations. For example, while looking at a page in a book that your child is familiar with, you might say, "Tell me what's happening in this picture." Open-ended prompts help increase children's attention to detail.

Dialogic Reading (continued)

W-prompts – These prompts usually begin with who, what, where, when, why, and how questions. Like open-ended prompts, W-prompts focus on the pictures in books. For example, you might say, "What's the name of this?" while pointing to an object in the book. W-questions teach children new vocabulary.

Distancing prompts – These prompts ask your child to relate the pictures or words in the book to experiences outside the book. For example, while looking at a book with a picture of animals on a farm, you might say something like, "Remember when we went to the animal park last week. Which of these animals did we see there?" Distancing prompts help children form a bridge between books and the real world, as well as help them with their verbal fluency, conversational abilities, and narrative skills.

Extending the activity

✤ After you've asked your child about stories and illustrations many times, encourage him or her to ask questions about the pictures in the book.

✤ Help your child make up his or her own oral story, copying the style of a favorite author. Help him or her include details to personalize the story.

What your child is practicing

When your child is answering questions about the pictures in a story, he or she is practicing paying close attention to illustrations and putting his or her thoughts into words. With a bit of encouragement, this can also become a time when your child practices using complete sentences to answer questions.

Author Studies

Targeted skill

Young children are expected to distinguish between the roles of author and illustrator. They are further expected to identify elements of authors' (and illustrators') style and characteristics.

Materials

◆ several books by the same author (such as Eric Carle, Marc Brown, or Kevin Henkes)

What to do

Read to your child two books by the same author. Talk with your child about the things that are similar in the two books. For example, if you're reading books by Marc Brown, talk about how D. W. always does something to be the annoying little sister or how Francine always seems to know more than Arthur. Continue to read and compare characters, settings, themes, and so on. Help your child understand the similarities between these books by the same author.

Extending the activity

❖ Studying various illustrators in the same manner helps your child understand the difference between the author (the one who has the idea and writes the words) and the illustrator (the one who creates the pictures or illustrations).

❖ If your child has trouble remembering details from the books, make a chart to record them. For example, write a character's name at the top of a sheet of paper. Then as you and your child read books with that character, add details about that character to the list. Reread the list with your child and talk about the way the character reacts in particular situations. As occasions arise, ask, "What would ___ do if ___ happened?" to bring your child's attention to the way the character would respond.

What your child is practicing

By focusing on a favorite author (or illustrator), your child is learning to remember details from a book and to relate those details to other books as well. Your child is learning that authors and illustrators have a particular style that makes them different from other authors or illustrators. As your child learns to read and write, he or she learns to develop an individual sense of style as well.

Newspaper Searches

Targeted skill

Young children are expected to recognize the letters of the alphabet, and later, sight words.

Materials

♦ sections from a daily newspaper

♦ highlighter pens

♦ piece of paper or index card

What to do

Tear out (or cut out) one page of the newspaper. Choose one letter of the alphabet and write its capital and lowercase forms on a piece of paper or index card. Remind your child of the letter's name and practice air-writing the letter (simply pretend to write the letter in the air). As you air-write the letter, describe what you are doing. For example, for *b*, say, "Straight line down, circle at the bottom." These little reminders help children remember how to write letters and how to recognize letters.

Challenge your child to find and highlight the letter you selected—and have him or her say the letter name each time it is highlighted. It is always a good idea to do the same work your child is doing, so take another newspaper page and highlight the selected letter as well, then ask your child to read the highlighted letters on your page of the paper.

Extending the activity

After your child reaches the point at which he or she can easily find the identified letter in newspaper print, ask your child to look for commonly used words, such as *the*, *and*, *is*, and *was*. These are called "sight words."

What your child is practicing

During Newspaper Searches, your child is practicing the skill of finding one specific bit of information from a page full of text. This early step of making sense of print is one of the pre-reading skills that help prepare your child for real reading.

Logos All Around

Targeted skill

Young children are expected to recognize beginning letters and associate them with the sound they make.

Materials

♦ logos clipped from advertisements or wrappers, paper bags, napkins, and so on from fast-food restaurants

What to do

All around us, there are opportunities for even the youngest learner to read, and he or she doesn't even have to know any letters! As you pass McDonald's, point to the golden arches and say, "Mmm, McDonald's. That's the sound of the letter *m*." After that, each time you pass McDonald's, ask your child to read the name on the sign. Soon, your child will associate the logo with the /m/ sound. We are surrounded by print in the mail, on newspapers, on cans and boxes, on television and signs. By showing your child how to associate beginning sounds with familiar logos, you are helping him or her learn the letters and their sounds.

Extending the activity

✤ Start by calling your child's attention to signs and the sounds that the beginning letters make. When your child is familiar with these, point out the words on the cereal box and describe the difference in the logo on a box of Cheerios and a box of Fruit Loops.

✤ Cut logos out of magazines and newspapers or save them from fast-food restaurants. Glue or tape them to pieces of sturdy paper, creating a Logo Notebook. Encourage your child to leaf through the book, reading the logos to you.

What your child is practicing

Print surrounds us. In our homes we have advertisements, newspapers, and books, along with various kinds of packaging—boxes, cans, and so on. As you drive through the neighborhood, your child sees billboard advertisements and marquees. This offers an opportunity for your child to begin to read logos and associate print with reading. By celebrating these successes, your child is encouraged to "read more" and thus the accuracy improves.

Reading the Coupons

Targeted skill

Young children are expected to name and identify each letter of the alphabet and to understand that written words are composed of letters that represent sounds.

Materials

◆ a collection of coupons from magazines or the Sunday newspaper

What to do

This activity is one that the whole family can do together. Gather an assortment of coupons and ask your child to help you sort them before going shopping. Show your child how to find the name of the product on the coupon (it's usually in larger or bolder print).

As your child identifies the product, help him or her connect the beginning letter with the product's name. Do this aloud so that your child learns to associate the letter's name with its form.

Extending the activity

✤ Encourage your child to group the coupons by category, such as cleaning products, breakfast food, and pets. As your child becomes more familiar with the task, ask him or her to make even more precise groupings. For example, help your child further divide the "cleaning products" category into "washing clothes," "cleaning the bathtub," "washing the car," and so on.

✤ Staple together 26 blank pages and write one letter of the alphabet on each one. Give your child glue and help him or her glue the coupons on the appropriate pages. This activity could also be done with 26 small envelopes.

Reading the Coupons *(continued)*

❖ Through this activity your child is learning the letters and their sounds, but you can also help him or her with other skills. Letting your child clip the coupons out with scissors gives him or her an opportunity to practice fine-motor coordination. To practice math skill, ask him or her to say the numerals on the coupons and perhaps organize them in numerical order or group them with like numbers together.

❖ If you have more coupons than your family can use, consider sharing them with other friends or family members who might use them. Help your child prepare envelopes to hold the extra coupons and perhaps even address the envelopes to mail them.

What your child is practicing

Children need many, many experiences with letters before they remember them. Incorporating this letter practice with a family activity helps your child understand the reason for learning the letters of the alphabet. It also offers him or her a real-world reason for learning letters and their sounds.

Driving for Signs

Targeted skill

Young children are expected to name and identify each letter of the alphabet, both the capital and lowercase forms. Further, they are expected to learn that written words are composed of letters that represent sounds. They are also expected to learn the consonant and vowel sounds for these letters.

Materials

◆ signs that you observe

What to do

Since many families spend a lot of time outside of their home, riding in either public transportation or private cars, it makes sense to use this time productively. Familiar street signs often intrigue young children, even though they do not know what the words on the signs say.

Call your child's attention to a familiar sign, such as a stop sign. Talk to him or her about the features of that sign. You might discuss the sign's shape, the letters, any letters that are repeated, the sign's colors, and so on. You might contrast the capital and lowercase letters on the sign.

Your child can also learn familiar words from a sign. Street signs display the names of streets; direction signs often incorporate direction words such as *right* or *left*; traffic signs display words such as *slow* and *turn*; speed-limit signs teach numerals.

Extending the activity

✤ When you return home, ask your child to write down the letters that he or she saw. Make signs to represent favorites. Your child might make traffic signs to use in his or her playtime.

✤ Ask your child to count the number of times you see a particular sign in the course of a trip. While stopped in traffic, notice letters that are repeated in a given sign.

What your child is practicing

This activity focuses your child's attention on letters and words that he or she sees every day. Calling your child's attention to signs helps him or her associate letter names with shapes (and possibly sounds as well).

Clapping the Word

Targeted skill

Young children are expected to learn how to divide words into parts, or syllables. Dividing words into syllables is part of a set of skills that educators refer to as phonological awareness. It is one of the steps in learning to read.

What to do

This is a game that you can play with your child almost anywhere. It is simple: Just say a word slowly and clap your hands once for each syllable. If the word is *cat*, you clap once. If the word is *bedroom*, you clap once when you say "bed" and once when you say "room." If the word is *caterpillar*, you'll clap four times—once for "cat," once for "er," once for "pil," and once for "lar."

Children usually like to clap their own name, the names of family members, and the names of friends. Beyond that, clap the syllables for familiar words such as things you eat, favorite toys, and places you go together.

If your child seems to have difficulty hearing the syllables within a word, try this: Have your child place a hand under his or her jaw. The jaw usually drops for each syllable. This physical motion makes identifying syllables a bit more concrete.

Extending the activity

Once your child can hear the syllables in most words without assistance, you can move on to the more advanced skill of phonemic awareness. Rather than listening for syllables, encourage your child to listen for phonemes (letter sounds). Start with simple three-letter words in which each sound is clear, for example, *mom*, *dad*, *cat*, *dog*, *bed*, and so on. Rather than clapping letter sounds, use a different motion, such as tapping your fingers on your knee.

What your child is practicing

Phonological awareness is a group of skills that includes rhyming, alliteration, sentence segmentation, word segmentation, and phonemic awareness. Phonological awareness is important as children learn to read.

Hearing the number of syllables in a word is second nature to adults, but not for young children. Children need lots and lots of practice saying words aloud and recognizing the syllables. Clapping out the syllables helps make them more concrete for children.

One of These Things Is Not Like the Others

Targeted skill

Young children are expected to recognize the difference between letters as well as to name and identify each letter of the alphabet.

Materials

◆ index cards

◆ pencil

What to do

This activity helps your child learn to look closely at letters to see what is different (and the same) about them. Cut an index card into three parts. Write the same letter on two of the pieces and a different letter on the third. Ask your child to turn away from the playing area while you arrange the pieces in a row. Ask him or her to look at the pieces and identify the letter that is different. Say, "Find one of these things that is not like the others." When your child identifies the different letter, call his or her attention to the similarities and differences between the letters. Continue with other letters.

Extending the activity

✤ This activity works well for comparing rhyming words. Write two rhyming words on two cards and on the third card write a word that does not rhyme. Ask your child to find the card that is different and to explain why.

✤ This activity can also be played with picture cards that relate to other language concepts. For example, play this game to find words that have the same middle or ending sound, words that have the same beginning blend, or words that have the same number of letters.

One of These Things Is Not Like the Others (continued)

❖ Common objects found in the kitchen or garage are often good for this activity. Make it into a "magic trick" by covering the objects with a small scarf or piece of fabric and saying, "Abracadabra!" when you remove it.

❖ The activity can be used for all sorts of comparisons. For example, displaying two red objects and one yellow object helps your child's color recognition. Displaying two pictures of pizza and one of a carrot helps your child learn to categorize food groups. Displaying a picture of a train, a car, and a banana requires him or her to categorize objects according to their function.

More questions to ask

Ask your child how he or she would change the objects to make them all match. Challenge him or her to find other small toys that could replace the object that does not match.

What your child is practicing

When your child can recognize small differences between letters or pictures, he or she is learning to look closely at similar objects. Your child is also learning to notice similarities and differences and to explain them.

ABC Collection Bags

Targeted skill

Young children are expected to name and identify each letter of the alphabet as well as to isolate sounds within a word and associate a letter with each of those sounds.

Materials

◆ collection of small toys or trinkets

◆ 26 resealable plastic bags or small boxes (the ones bank checks come in work well)

◆ marker

What to do

Most children have a collection of small toys or other trinkets that seem to accumulate in the bottom of the toy box. Turn these into a letter/sound activity for your child.

Label 26 resealable plastic bags (or tubs or small boxes) with the letters of the alphabet. Help your child sort through the small toys, emphasizing the beginning sound of each one. Help him or her place each one in the appropriately labeled bag.

Extending the activity

✤ After a few objects are sorted, select two or three bags with letters that are familiar to your child. Mix those objects and ask your child to sort them back into the correct bag. Help him or her say the beginning sound of each object and remind him or her of the letter associated with that sound.

ABC Collection Boxes *(continued)*

✜ Finding small objects for this activity can involve all family members. Small toys that are used as birthday party favors or purchased at dollar stores make great additions to the collection. Assign family members a letter and challenge them to find small objects that match that letter. Help your child be the final judge of which objects go in which bags, reminding him or her that there can be numerous names for the same object, such as dog, puppy, or terrier.

More questions to ask

Ask your child to create rhyming words by changing the first sound in a word. For example, if one of the objects is a toy boat, you and your child could change the /b/ sound to a /g/ to create *goat*, to /n/ to create *note*, and so on.

What your child is practicing

Learning which letter goes with which sound can be a confusing task for young children. By associating words with the same beginning sound, your child learns that the same sounds and letters are used over and over for different words.

Stretching the Words

Targeted skill

Young children are expected to identify and isolate the beginning and/or final letters in a word as well as to blend sounds to create a word.

Materials

♦ large rubber bands, pieces of elastic, or strips of stretchy fabric

What to do

Usually the first reading strategy that young children learn is to "sound out." Sounding out words is helpful in many cases, but learning to read goes beyond that. Stretching a rubber band or piece of elastic is a concrete way that young children can see how letters "stretch" to make a word.

First, point out a word that your child might be having trouble with or is just beginning to learn. Then, suggest that he or she knows every sound in that word and that the next step is to blend the sounds together. Give your child the rubber band and ask him or her to slowly say the sounds as he or she stretches the band. Have your child continue to say the sounds and stretch the band several times. Praise your child as he or she begins to blend the sounds to create the word.

Alternatively, take the rubber band and stretch it for your child without saying any sounds. Ask your child to say the word as you stretch the band. Make this a game by stretching the rubber band slowly at first and then stretching it quickly. Expect your child to match your speed.

Stretching the Words (continued)

Extending the activity

❖ As your child becomes accustomed to this activity, the simple suggestion to "stretch it out" may be enough to remind him or her of this strategy. Stretching it out goes beyond sounding it out because the child already knows the sounds and just needs to blend them together.

❖ Some children benefit from moving the letters as they say them. Write the letters of a particular word on small (one-inch-square) pieces of paper. Ask your child to push them together as he or she says the word.

❖ Use root words to create other words. For example, start with the word *go* and "stretch" it to make *goes* or *going*. Other words that work well for this activity include action words such as *run, jump, hop, leap,* and *come*.

❖ Some children benefit from using the strategy of "say it on your arm." It is similar to stretching the rubber band, but the child simply indicates the shoulder area for the first sound in a word, the elbow area for the middle sound, and the area near the wrist for the final sound. Ask your child to hold out his or her arm and use the opposite hand to indicate the various areas as he or she slowly says the word. Encourage him or her to move the opposite hand faster down the arm as he or she learns to blend the sounds together quickly.

What your child is practicing

Your child is learning to do more than sound out words in these activities. He or she is learning how letters mesh together to make a new, or different, sound. Your child is learning to look beyond the first letter in a word and discover the other letters. Doing so not only helps your child learn to read but also helps him or her develop self-confidence as he or she makes these discoveries.

Labeling Pictures
Letter by Letter

Targeted skill

Young children are expected to learn phonics, an essential part of learning to read.

Materials

♦ drawing paper

♦ crayons or markers

What to do

You and your child begin by each drawing your own picture. Then model labeling different objects in your picture. If, for example, you've drawn a typical "house with tree" picture, say, "I am going to write a label for my house." Say "house" very slowly, emphasizing each letter sound. It might sound like /h/ /au/ /s/. After saying the word a couple of times, say /h/ and write an "h" beside the house, then say /au/ and write an "o" after the "h," then say /s/ and write an "s" after the "o." Decide to label something else in the picture, perhaps a flower. The letters you write might be "flr." In this activity, it is important to write only the letters for the sounds you emphasize, or hear. This is called "phonetic spelling." This is not the time to emphasize correct spelling.

After you've written a couple of labels, encourage your child to identify and label something on his or her picture. Repeat the word your child says, saying it very slowly. For example, say /k/ /a/ /t/, for *cat*. In this word, each of the letters can be clearly heard. That is not always true. Don't try to make your child "hear" something that he or she really doesn't hear. Some children write only the first letter of each word, while others hear only the first and last sounds. These are natural stages, and children will progress to hearing most of the sounds in a word in time.

Extending the activity

Encourage your child to use phonetic spelling to write lots of things: grocery lists, thank-you notes, reminders, notes to family members, and so on.

What your child is practicing

Most of the time when adults think of phonics, they think of "sounding out" unknown words when reading. Teachers call this decoding, or figuring out an unknown word by using letter-sound correspondence. This activity is really *en*coding. Your child is writing the letters that represent the sounds he or she is saying aloud.

Word Families

Targeted skill

By creating word families, young children are learning the characteristics of rhyming words and learning to identify the beginning and ending of a word. They are also learning that individual letters (and their sounds) can be changed to make new words.

Materials

♦ paper

♦ marker or pencil

What to do

It can be confusing for young children that changing the first sound of a word creates an entirely new word. On a piece of paper, write a common, familiar word such as "cat." Under that word, write "_at." Then ask your child to think of another letter that would make a new word. Continue in this manner to create a long list of words (such as *fat, hat, mat, pat, rat, sat, bat*). Ask your child to reread the words.

Then (or on another day, depending on your child's interest) continue the lesson with another familiar word family. Common word families include *-ad, -an, -et, -it,* and *-op.*

Extending the activity

❖ Be sure to include two-letter beginning sounds. For example, when working with the *-ap* family, use such initial sounds as /cl/, /fl/, and /ch/.

❖ You can use simple flipbooks to reinforce this idea. Cut several index cards in thirds. Use a stapler to attach three or four (depending on your child's ability) of these small pieces to one end of a full-size index card. On each small piece, write a different initial letter. On the full-size card, write the ending. Then flip the small pieces to reveal a new word. As your child thinks of more initial sounds for a particular family, encourage him or her to add more small pieces to create more words.

Word Families *(continued)*

❖ Point out the similarities between word families. That is, help focus your child's attention on the vowel sound of similar words. For example, compare the -*an* family with the -*en* family. Compare the number of words that are in each family and check to see if all possible combinations have been identified.

What your child is practicing

Young children are surprised by the idea that simply changing the first sound of a word creates a new word. Understanding this idea helps your child learn to read a lot more words quickly and ties in to learning to rhyme words as well.

Word Wall Go Fish

Targeted skill

Young children are expected to recognize sight words quickly.

Materials

◆ small index cards

◆ markers or crayons

◆ list of sight words that the class is learning

What to do

In the classroom, sight words are posted on the Word Wall. Five new sight words are added every week. Attached is the list of sight words on our Word Wall.

Write each word on the list on four index cards to create the deck for Word Wall Go Fish. It is played like any other game of Go Fish.

To play:

1. Deal six cards to each player, then place the remainder of the cards facedown between the players. Turn one card faceup.

2. Player 1 selects a sight word in his or her hand and asks any player if he or she has that particular word. If the player does, he or she must give it to Player 1. Player 1 can continue asking other players for specific cards until one of the players does not have the requested card and responds, "Go fish." Player 1 then takes the card on top of the remainder pile.

3. The first player to collect all four cards with the same sight word wins.

Extending the activity

Work with your child to create the sight-word cards for this game. Writing a sight word four times helps reinforce that particular word for your child.

What your child is practicing

Young children must learn lots of different skills to become good readers. One of these skills is memorizing sight words. Words like *one*, *the*, and *said* cannot be sounded out. They must be memorized. Your child is much more likely to practice reading sight words by playing a game than by reading flash cards or writing the words over and over.

Drawing the Story

Targeted skill

Young children are expected to determine the purpose for listening to a story, such as to get information, to solve problems, or just for enjoyment. Also, they are expected to retell the order of important events in stories as well as understand the structure of simple stories.

Materials

◆ paper

◆ drawing materials such as crayons, felt-tip markers, or colored pencils

What to do

After sharing a simple book or story with your child, ask your child to draw an event from the story. Encourage him or her to include as many details as possible. For example, if the book emphasized the color of the character's hair, then your child should include that in the drawing.

Discuss with your child the details that are included. Talk about how the characters might have felt or why the particular actions occurred.

Extending the activity

✚ Have your child draw more than one picture of a favorite story and assemble them into a "book" about that story. Make a construction-paper cover and staple the pictures together. Ask your child to compare the text with the collected drawings.

✚ Your child can draw a favorite part, the main idea, the funniest thing that happened, the saddest thing that happened, and so on.

Drawing the Story *(continued)*

❖ Your child can make a mural-type drawing to represent all the details of the story. For example, if the story is about a character's day, then divide a large piece of paper into three parts, labeling them morning, afternoon, and evening. Then help your child draw what happened at each time during the day.

❖ Asking your child to orally retell the events in the story helps him or her understand the story. Ask questions such as, "What happened next?" or "What happened first?" to focus his or her attention. Begin to ask the why and how questions as well, such as, "Why did ___ do that?" or "How did that action change the story?"

What your child is practicing

Learning to represent events in a story by drawing them is a first step to understanding and retelling stories. Children who have difficulty with comprehension or remembering details often benefit from drawing a picture that represents what they've heard.

Drawing What You Know

Targeted skill

Young children are expected to record their ideas and reflections. By using drawing to do so, they are forming a foundation for learning to write these things later on.

Materials

◆ paper

◆ drawing materials such as crayons, felt-tip markers, or colored pencils

What to do

As you share a story with your child, read the text until just before you come to the climax—the "exciting part" or a part that is important to the ending of the story. Ask your child to "draw what you know." Help your child recall details from the story that lead up to this important point in the story. After the drawing is complete, read the rest of the story and compare your child's drawing to what happened in the story.

Extending the activity

✜ Your child could draw attributes of a character. For example, if a character is particularly kind, the drawing might include several kind things the character did in the story.

More questions to ask

Ask your child to make predictions about the story. He or she can draw these predictions and then compare them to the actual story. Emphasize that these are simply "predictions" about what might happen, and that any differences are not things that your child got "wrong."

What your child is practicing

Your child is recognizing that he or she knows facts from a story rather than just listening without any involvement. Also, learning to represent what he or she knows by drawing helps prepare your child for learning to read.

Retellings

> ## Targeted skill
>
> Young children are expected to retell or act out the order of important events in a story, develop vocabulary by listening to and discussing familiar stories, and identify words that name persons, places, and things as well as words that name actions.

What to do

Your child benefits from retelling events in chronological order. Practicing this skill with common events helps your child do this later with stories he or she has read or listened to.

The first time you help your child with the activity, be sure to point out the events prior to asking your child to retell them. For example, point out the way he or she gets dressed in the morning as each task is accomplished. Then, later in the day, ask your child to tell three things he or she did in order to get dressed.

As your child becomes better at doing this, the preparation work will not be as important. Encourage your child to retell common events, such as setting the table, ordering ice cream, taking a bath, or putting on pajamas.

Extending the activity

❖ Encourage your child to use proper terms to describe the events that occur. Help him or her use new vocabulary words as well.

❖ Some children benefit from using objects in the retellings. You might draw three or four boxes (about 4-inch-square). Then ask your child to draw a different event in each box. For example, to describe coming home from school, your child might draw walking in the door, putting the backpack on the table, hanging up a coat, and getting a snack. Then cut the boxes apart and challenge your child to arrange them in order.

Retellings *(continued)*

❖ Ask your child to organize photographs of a family outing in the order in which they happened. Or take photos of a common event and have your child arrange them in order while orally telling the story.

More questions to ask

❖ Asking, "What happened next?" or "What happened before?" helps your child learn that events occur in a sequence.

❖ Introduce some "what if" ideas to a story. Ask your child to describe how the story would change if a particular thing was different or did not occur.

What your child is practicing

Retelling events helps your child understand the idea of sequence and the elements (character, setting, problem, and solution) of a story. Often it is easier to identify these in something he or she has participated in rather than in a story read to him or her.

Fact or Fantasy?

Targeted skill

Good readers evaluate meaning as they read. Learning to distinguish between fact and fantasy is part of the reading process.

What to do

Young children often blur the line between fact and fantasy. They often have imaginary playmates and make up stories while they are playing. Learning to recognize these differences is a part of maturing and growing up.

In informal situations, introduce the idea of what makes a fact. Point out to your child that a fact is something you can prove, such as by seeing an event or by touching an object. Discuss examples of this with your child. For instance, it is a fact that he drank milk for breakfast and a fantasy that he drank coffee. Continue to bring this up with concrete examples, such as during dinner, at playtime, or while riding in the car.

Extending the activity

✤ Help your child recognize things that are opposites. For example, identify a cold drink and ask him or her to give an example of a hot drink, or ask him or her to contrast something that is funny and something that is sad. Other opposites include top/bottom, in/out, on/off, and front/back.

✤ Some children have trouble making up stories or thinking of fanciful things. Encourage your child's imagination by extending conversations to include fanciful things. For example, say, "Wow! That is a big truck. It is as big as a skyscraper!" Then discuss with your child how that was an exaggeration and help him or her come up with a more reasonable description.

✤ Some children use a doll or favorite stuffed animal to respond to this activity. It is often easier for children to tap into their imagination by letting the doll or stuffed animal talk.

What your child is practicing

It is often difficult for young children to distinguish between something that is true and something false, fact and fantasy, real and make-believe. Practicing this skill in a structured way helps your child transfer it to everyday life.

Sequencing Events

Targeted skill

Young children are expected to use prior knowledge to make sense of texts. This requires being able to predict what comes before and after a given event. Activities such as this one help them learn to place events in order.

Materials

♦ index cards

♦ crayons, felt-tip markers, pencils

What to do

This activity involves drawing pictures of events on index cards, mixing the cards up, and reorganizing them in the order that they occurred. First, help your child draw a sequence of events on several index cards. You might ask him or her to record the events of a particular day, a special occasion (like a birthday party, family picnic, or other such event), or a family vacation. Then turn the cards facedown and mix them up. Turn the cards faceup and ask your child to find the first event that occurred. He or she places that event to the left of the playing area. Then he or she continues to pick the events in the order they occurred, placing them in the correct order.

Be sure to discuss the events as your child is arranging them. Comments like, "Yes, the kite is still on the ground in this picture so it goes before the one where the kite is flying," help your child understand the relationship between events.

Sequencing Events *(continued)*

Extending the activity

✤ If your child seems overwhelmed, simplify the task. Ask him or her to draw only three events and order them as "first, next, and last." For example, brushing teeth involves putting the toothpaste on the toothbrush, brushing, and putting the brush and toothpaste away.

✤ You and your child can make two copies of each event and play Concentration. Shuffle the cards and place them facedown in a grid pattern. Play begins with the first player turning over two cards in search of a match. If the cards match, the player removes them from the game. If not, the player turns them back over, and the next player goes. The game is over when all cards are matched.

✤ Acting out a series of events can be a fun family activity. Select an event, make the cards for it, and arrange them in order before dramatizing the events. Help your child think of actions to match each card. This can be as simple or complex as you want.

✤ Be sure to use words such as *first, next, last* or *first, second, third* when doing this activity. Other transition words such as *then, after that, later,* and *in a while* are also appropriate. Using these words over and over helps your child understand their meaning.

> ### What your child is practicing
>
> When your child places events in order, he or she is learning to act out or retell important events in a story.

Acrostic Poem

Targeted skill

Young children are expected to master several skills associated with creating acrostic poems, such as identifying and isolating the initial sound of a word; understanding various literary forms by distinguishing among such types as stories, poems, and information books; and writing to record ideas and reflections.

Materials

♦ paper   ♦ pencil

What to do

Begin by helping your child write each letter in his or her first name vertically on the left side of the paper, spacing the letters evenly up and down the page. Talk with your child about his or her personal qualities. Write a quality for each letter in his or her name. Then read the poem with your child.

Extending the activity

✤ You and your child can create acrostic poems for last names, other family members' names, pets' names, neighbors' names, and so on.

✤ You can narrow the scope of an acrostic poem by limiting the horizontal words to a category, such as foods, names of cars, or vegetables.

✤ Acrostic poems designed for grandparents or aunts and uncles can become treasured gifts. Help your child focus on aspects of that person that your child especially appreciates, such as *greatness, grins, gentle, giving, glorious, gorgeous,* or *good* for the *g* in *grandma.* Your child could write the poem on paper with an attractive border.

✤ Ask your child to defend his or her choice of a particular quality. Help him or her learn to support his or her decisions with reasons.

What your child is practicing

Your child is learning to associate a letter's sound with a word that begins with that letter and to make the best choice from several possibilities.

Lists, Lists, Lists

Targeted skill

Young children are expected to learn to distinguish different forms of texts, such as lists, newsletters, and signs, and the functions they serve; name and identify each letter of the alphabet; and learn and apply letter-sound correspondences of a set of consonants and vowels to begin to read.

Materials

◆ paper

◆ pencil

What to do

Enlist your child's help as you create lists in your family's day-to-day life. Making grocery lists is a good way to start. Give your child some paper (a notepad works well for this) and pencil and encourage him or her to write down the needed items. Have your child bring the list along when you go to the store and read you the list as you shop.

You may have to show your child examples of a list. Use lists that you have made or some that you find in advertisements. Show your child that the words are listed vertically. If you want, show your child how to number the list along the left side of the page.

Extending the activity

✤ Lists can be made for many different things, such as places to go for a holiday, gifts desired, names of fellow classmates, lists of family members, a to-do list for Saturday's tasks, or books to read.

✤ Adding a quick sketch to a word on the list can help your child remember what that word represents.

Lists, Lists, Lists *(continued)*

Other things to do

✤ Obtain a paper pad made especially for list making. Often these are lined and numbered along the left side. Make this the special list-making paper for your family.

✤ If your child enjoys this activity, you might show him or her how to categorize the list. For example, the canned goods and dairy products on a grocery list could be put under separate headings.

What your child is practicing

Repeated experiences in writing a list of frequently used words gives your child the practice he or she needs in order to learn the necessary letters and their sounds.

Writing Reminders

Targeted skill

This activity encourages young children to take part in language activities that extend their vocabulary and conceptual knowledge. They learn that print represents spoken language and proceeds from left to right across the page.

Materials

♦ paper

♦ pencil

What to do

Enlist your child's help in writing a reminder for an actual task or create an opportunity to do this. While you are working at another task, say, for example, "Hey! I just remembered that we are supposed to take the blue book back to the library. Will you use that paper on the counter to write a reminder and we'll tape it by the door to remind us?" Then help your child write by stretching out the sounds in the word and referring to the letters your child needs to write the message.

Accept the message as written at your child's ability level. Younger children might write "bl bk" or "libr" to represent "blue book" and "library." Ask your child to read the message and perhaps reread it to another family member. Then tape it by the door at your child's eye level. Say, "That reminder you wrote will help us remember to get the blue book when we go on our errands." Then, when it is time to do the task, show your child how the reminder helped by referring to it. Say, "Oh, I am so glad that reminder is by the door. We almost forgot the blue book, but now we see the reminder and we can take it with us."

When you write yourself a reminder and refer to it in front of your child, you are serving as a role model for reading and writing. When you involve your child in this activity, you are helping him or her learn important skills.

Writing Reminders *(continued)*

Extending the activity

✣ Involve your child in writing reminders for necessary tasks. Enlist his or her help to write a reminder to brush his or her teeth and place it on the bathroom mirror, to turn off the bedroom light and place it by the light switch, and so on.

✣ Encourage your child to use reminders as he or she plays. Make sure your child has paper and pencil within easy reach of the play area. Reminders can be created for dolls or action figures.

✣ Give your child his or her own scratch pad. Make it a practice to refer to it when there are tasks to be done. Suggest that your child use the special pad to record them.

✣ Using a computer, you can make scratch paper with your child's name at the top or insert familiar logos. Divide a page into four sections (two at the top and two at the bottom). Type the name or logo at the top of each section, print, and cut apart.

✣ Make it a part of your family's routine to "check the reminders" before beginning a task. Involve your child as much as possible in this routine so that he or she learns the importance of writing.

What your child is practicing

Your child is learning more conventions of writing, such as that writing proceeds from left to right, that words represent thoughts written down, and that writing is used for a specific purpose. Additionally, he or she is learning organizational skills and ways of remembering things.

Writing Thank-You Notes

Targeted skill

Young children are expected to write notes, reminders, labels, and so on as they learn to connect the letters with the sounds they make. This is how they learn to spell, read, and write.

Materials

♦ paper

♦ crayon, felt-tip marker, or pencil

What to do

Receiving a gift can be an opportunity for your child to practice his or her writing skills. This activity can be as simple or involved as you wish.

To begin, explain to your child that since he or she likes a particular gift, he or she could write a letter of thanks to the person who gave the gift. Provide paper (it could be folded note cards, colored paper, or drawing paper) and something to write with. Help your child sound out words to express the thanks. Once again, this can be as simple as "Thak u" or something more complicated.

Ask your child to sign the card, and then place it in an envelope. Address the envelope, add a stamp, and put it in the mail to help your child understand the process of posting a letter.

Extending the activity

❖ There are many opportunities to write letters. Grandparents appreciate receiving an "I love you" note or a card to celebrate a holiday. Handmade cards are always appreciated.

Writing Thank-you Notes *(continued)*

✤ One fun way to do this activity is to take photographs of your child holding the gift. Your child can write the thank-you note on the back of the photo. Tuck it into an envelope and mail it.

✤ Another alternative that works well at birthday parties is to take a picture of your child and the gift-giving child together as your child receives his or her gift. Then your child can write the thanks on the back of that picture and send it to the giver.

✤ Be sure to talk with your child about what to say on the card. He or she can extend the writing to include descriptive words or could describe how the gift has been enjoyed.

What your child is practicing

Not only is your child practicing many language arts skills, but he or she is also practicing social skills, such as being gracious.

Writing Messages

Targeted skill

Young children are expected to learn that writing is used for a reason and that writing represents thoughts or spoken words written down.

Materials

♦ paper

♦ pencil

What to do

Writing messages with your child seems a natural thing to do after creating lists and writing reminders. Messages are an effective way to communicate and offer information to others.

When you and your child are leaving the house, ask him or her to write a message to other family members telling them where you are going or at what time you will return. Encourage your child to use his or her developing writing skills and help him or her "stretch" out the words to find the sounds. Leave the message on the table or other noticeable place. Encourage other family members to comment on how the message helped them.

Extending the activity

✤ Make sure that there are paper and pencil near your child's play area or in his or her room. Encourage your child to use them during play.

✤ Invent things to do with messages. Instead of talking, pass quick notes back and forth. For example, when your child asks you a yes-or-no question, grab a pencil and write your answer. If your child asks for more information about a subject, tell him or her to write the question. Then respond with a written answer.

Writing Messages (continued)

❖ Help your child participate in writing messages to people outside of the immediate family. For example, your child can write a message to the neighbor asking him to watch your house while you are out of town. Of course, you may need to help your neighbor understand what your child has written!

❖ Young children enjoy messages that elicit emotions. Among the easiest are "I love you" messages, but do not forget messages that inform ("We are going to the zoo") or surprise ("I see you"). Encourage your child to read these messages from you and write more on his or her own.

What your child is practicing

Many parents and caregivers place messages in their child's lunch or pocket. These messages surprise the child and remind him or her of the family. By teaching your child to write messages, he or she is learning that words can have a powerful effect on people. When your child gives you a note that expresses love and receives a hug in response, he or she learns the power of words.

Introduction to Alphabet and Numeral Activities

The following pages contain activities that help children remember the letters *A* to *Z* and the numerals 1 to 10. Some children seem to learn letter names (and the associated sounds) and numeral names (and the value they represent) rather quickly. Other children need many more experiences. Not every child makes the same connection between the abstract squiggles he or she made in an activity and what we call letters and numbers.

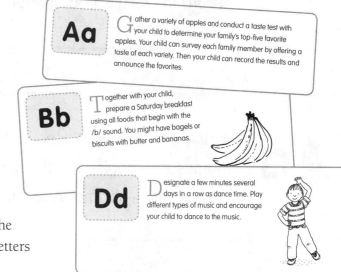

Aa — Gather a variety of apples and conduct a taste test with your child to determine your family's top-five favorite apples. Your child can survey each family member by offering a taste of each variety. Then your child can record the results and announce the favorites.

Bb — Together with your child, prepare a Saturday breakfast using all foods that begin with the /b/ sound. You might have bagels or biscuits with butter and bananas.

Dd — Designate a few minutes several days in a row as dance time. Play different types of music and encourage your child to dance to the music.

Many children need some kind of "anchor experience" to help them remember this knowledge. Of course, not every child remembers *A* simply because of apples or *B* because of balls. Some children remember A because of a friend named Aaron or because of their fascination with astronauts. In this light, we present families with a few anchor experiences for each letter or numeral to use with their children.

There are several ways to use these experiences with your class. You might select the activities for the letters or numerals that you are presenting in class and attach them to your weekly family communication. You could simply attach the activities to the bottom of your family communication before photocopying it. Or you may send the activities home only with those children who are struggling with remembering certain letters or numbers. At a family meeting, you might set up stations so that families can do the activities with their children. A classroom volunteer or tutor could use these activities with small groups of children. There are many possibilities.

Often, families want to help their children at home but do not know exactly what to do. With your guidance, they'll feel capable of "doing the right thing" with their child. As well, they usually appreciate specific suggestions of activities to do that will help their child.

 Gather a variety of apples and conduct a taste test with your child to determine your family's top-five favorite apples. Your child can survey each family member by offering a taste of each variety. Then your child can record the results and announce the favorites.

 Using a map, find places in the world with names that begin with the short-*a* sound, such as Antarctica, Alabama, Arizona, and Afghanistan.

 Some animals, such as anaconda and alligator, have names that begin with the short-*a* sound. After researching these, help your child draw an illustration of each one and write a capital and lowercase letter beside the drawing.

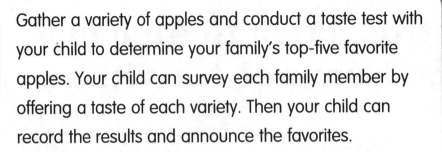 Use aluminum foil to make a sculpture. Show your child how to crumple the foil to create animals whose names begin with the short-*a* sound, such as an ant or an alligator.

 Just-Right Homework Activities for PreK–K © 2009 by Diffily & Sassman, Scholastic Teaching Resources

Bb Together with your child, prepare a Saturday breakfast using all foods with names that begin with the /b/ sound. You might have bagels or biscuits with butter or bananas.

Bb Take different-size balls outside and practice bouncing them, repeating the phrase "bouncing the ball" over and over. Each time emphasize the /b/ sound of the two words.

Bb Buy bubbles and share a few minutes blowing bubbles at each other.

Cc Use foods with names that begin with *c* to create a vegetable-and-dip platter. Enlist your child's help to prepare cauliflower, carrots, cabbage, corn, cucumber, cantaloupe, and so on. Serve these foods for dinner with cupcakes or cones of ice cream for dessert.

Cc Use construction paper to cut and glue a collage of colors, use colored corn to make a mosaic, or use clay to create coasters.

Cc Stack cans to make a sculpture.

Dd

Choose a weekend morning for a special "Doughnuts with Dad" breakfast.

Dd

Designate a few minutes several days in a row as dance time. Play different types of music and encourage your child to dance to the music.

Dd

Have a scavenger hunt to look for things with names that begin with the /d/ sound, such as a desk, dominoes, a dictionary, dice, a daughter, a duck, Delaware (if you have a map of the United States), a doctor, a dog, a dinosaur, or dishes.

Ee

Eat eggs for dinner! Cook hard-boiled eggs and make deviled eggs, beat eggs together to make scrambled eggs, or chop eggs to make egg salad sandwiches. Dye hard-boiled eggs and hide them for an egg hunt. Or have egg-rolling races with the dyed eggs.

Explore what might be an unfamiliar vegetable— eggplant! Buy an eggplant and let your child help you prepare it. Cook it and eat it with rice.

Lead your child in some motions with words that begin with the short-*e* sound. For example, you and your child could pretend to look over the edge of a cliff (or other high place), use an emery board to file fingernails, ride in an elevator, walk like an elephant, or embroider with a needle and thread.

 Go to the grocery store together and look at all the fish options. Buy a fish fillet, then bake it for a family meal.

 Cut out fish-shaped paper and write a capital *F* and lowercase *f* on each fish. Place a paper clip on each fish. Then tie string to a dowel rod or stick and place a magnet on the end of the string. A game of fishing and repeating the letter name and sound will reinforce remembering F.

 With paints, either finger paint or create fingerprints.

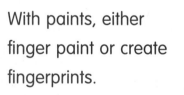

Gather gloves from all family members. Put them in a pile and help your child sort them. Then return them to the correct family member. Or have your child wear his or her gloves as simple household tasks are attempted. See if emptying trash bins, picking up the newspaper, putting away toys, and so on is easier or harder while wearing gloves.

Score a goal by kicking a soccer ball or throwing a baseball at a target. Yell "Goal!" each time your child scores.

Make garlic bread by spreading bread slices with butter and garlic. Serve with dinner.

Play Go and Stop in a fashion similar to Red Light, Green Light. Ask your child to move a distance from you. While you turn your back, your child advances toward you. At various intervals, yell "Stop!" as you turn around. If you see your child moving, he or she must return to the distant spot. Say "Go," turn around, and your child advances again. The object is for your child to reach you without getting caught.

 Just-Right Homework Activities for PreK–K © 2009 by Diffily & Sassman, Scholastic Teaching Resources

Hh Make a meal of hot dogs and hamburgers for family and friends.

Hh Create hats out of newspaper or some other materials.

Hh Create handprints with paint and small pieces of paper.

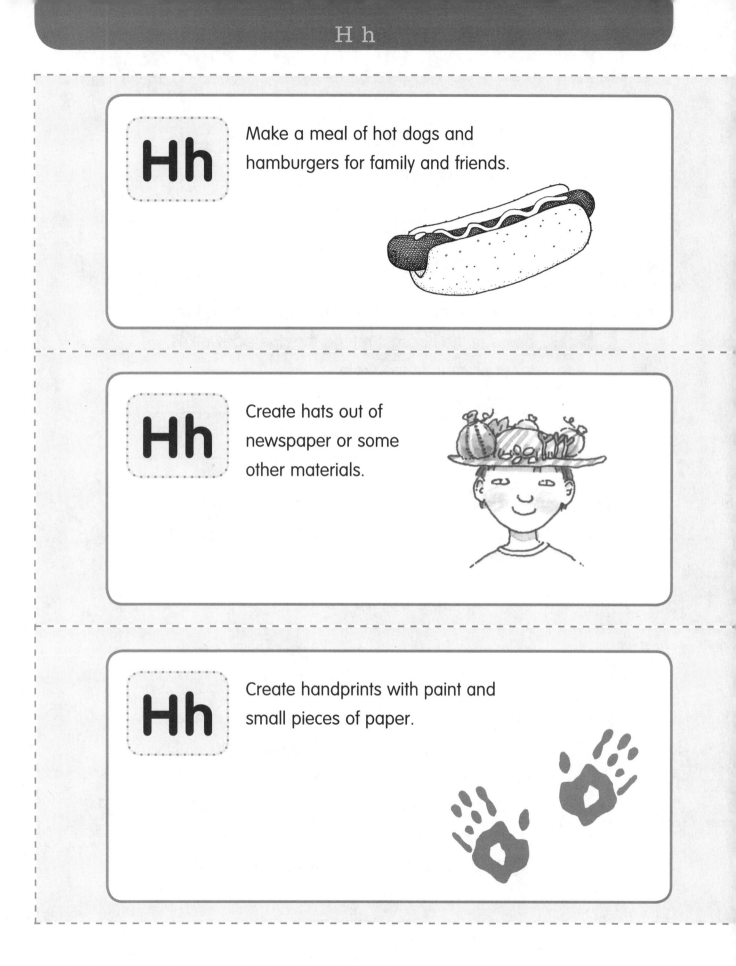

 Invite friends over for an ice-cream party. Or ice a cake with icing.

 Make icicles out of paper and tape them to the eaves of the house. Pretend that the sidewalk is icy or pretend to ice-skate.

 Build an igloo. Use sugar cubes, blocks, or boxes to construct an igloo. Or make ice sculptures using ice cubes on a towel.

 Compare the melting rates of ice. Freeze water in a plastic container to make a large block. Compare the melting rate of the large block with those of smaller cubes. Or place the same number of cubes in different locations—a warm spot, a cool spot, in the sun, in the shade. Observe the cubes to see which melts the fastest and which the slowest.

Jj

Memorizing the letter name and sound for *J* offers a good time for exercise. Together, do jumping jacks and chant, "J, J, Jumping Jacks."

Jj

Make a breakfast of foods with names that begin with *J*: juice, Jell-O, jam, and jelly.

Jj

Play with jump ropes or have a jumping jacks contest.

Kk Play kickball or simply kick a ball back and forth. Or go to an open area and fly kites.

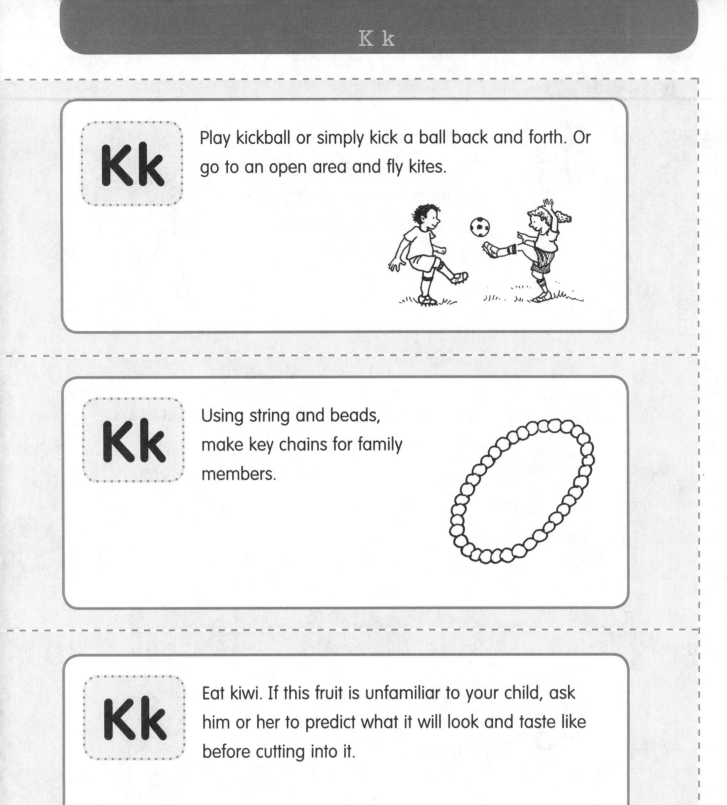

Kk Using string and beads, make key chains for family members.

Kk Eat kiwi. If this fruit is unfamiliar to your child, ask him or her to predict what it will look and taste like before cutting into it.

 Create a dinner of foods whose names begin with the letter *L*: lemonade, lasagna, and lettuce with lime juice.

 Have a limbo contest. Find a broom. Play party music. Take turns bending backward and walking under the broom handle. Lower the broom a little bit each round.

 Make leaf prints by collecting different-shape leaves and pressing the leaves into paint and then onto paper. Or place leaves between two sheets of wax paper and gently press them together with a warm iron. Be sure to closely supervise the use of the iron.

Chant the traditional rhyme "Miss Mary Mack" with your child. Add hand motions if you desire.

Miss Mary Mack, Mack, Mack
All dressed in black, black, black
With silver buttons, buttons, buttons
All down her back, back, back.

She asked her mother, mother, mother
For 50 cents, cents, cents
To see the elephants, elephants, elephants
Jump over the fence, fence, fence.

They jumped so high, high, high
They reached the sky, sky, sky
And didn't come back, back, back
Until the Fourth of July, ly, ly!

Eat foods with names that begin with the letter *M*. For dinner, have macaroni and meatballs or taste mangos, marshmallows, matzo, melba toast, mushrooms, and so on.

Make masks using paper plates and art supplies.

Nn String round cereal or hollow pasta to make necklaces.

Nn Make nachos (shredded cheese and/or refried beans on tortilla chips).

Nn Go to the library. Check out and read together *Noisy Nora* by Rosemary Wells.

 Celebrate "Orange Family Day" by asking all family members to wear orange. Tie an orange scarf on family pets as well.

 Eat orange foods, such as orange Jell-O, cantaloupe, cheese, and carrots.

 Cut out several sizes of octagons and ovals from construction paper. With your child, construct a collage using the shapes and glue.

Oo Listen to opera music. Some children's stories, such as *The Little Prince*, have been adapted to opera. Ask your child to imagine what is happening when the different instruments play. Ask him or her to move to the beat of the music.

Pp

Have a family pajama party and plan activities that emphasize words that begin with the /p/ sound. Make popcorn. Create puppets from paper bags. Play with play dough.

Pp

Experiment with foods that you don't normally eat, such as pineapple, pistachio nuts, peanut brittle, papaya, or peaches, or emphasize the beginning sound of some family favorites, such as pizza or popcorn. Repeating the word with emphasis on the beginning sound helps your child connect this letter and sound to a favorite food.

Pp

Check out "The Three Little Pigs" and read it aloud at bedtime. Each time the word *pig* appears in the book, emphasize the /p/ sound. Or count how many times the word is used in the book.

Qq Help your child make a crown out of construction paper or aluminum foil. Crown the female family members as "Queen for the Day."

Qq Cut small squares from various kinds of paper and glue them together to make a quilt.

Qq Paint a picture using Q-tips and paint.

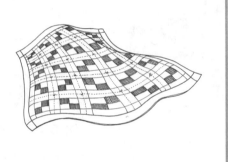

Just-Right Homework Activities for PreK–K © 2009 by Diffily & Sassman, Scholastic Teaching Resources

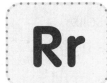

Go on a nature walk around the neighborhood with your child. Take along white paper and a few old crayons. Holding the crayon on its side, make rubbings of different things you find outside: leaves, rocks, tree bark, bricks, sidewalks, fences.

Cook ravioli for dinner.

Have a scavenger hunt and search for items that are red. Look for red apples, red tomatoes, a red wagon, a red crayon, a red rose, and so on.

Teach your child the tongue twister "She sells seashells by the seashore." Repeat the sentence several times. Then help your child repeat small segments of it until he or she can say it alone.

Fix lunch by making sandwiches with sunflower seeds sprinkled on top. Serve with squash soup.

When doing the laundry, enlist your child's help to sort socks. Give him or her all the socks to arrange into matching pairs. Then they can be put away in the sock drawer.

Sing "Itsy, Bitsy Spider," emphasizing the /s/ sound in *spider*, *spout*, and *sun*. Or play Simon Says, highlighting motions with an /s/ sound, such as sitting down, standing up, or spinning around.

 Have your child sculpt turtles from clay or play dough. As he or she works, encourage talk about turtles, stressing words that begin with the /t/ sound, such as turtle and tail.

 Go to the library and check out several alphabet books. Have your child find all the "T" pages and re-create his or her favorite "T" pages.

 Make a lunch of foods that begin with the letter *T*. You might consider stuffing tomatoes with tuna and drinking tea.

U u Go outside with umbrellas and pretend to walk in the rain. Or dance with them in a pretend show.

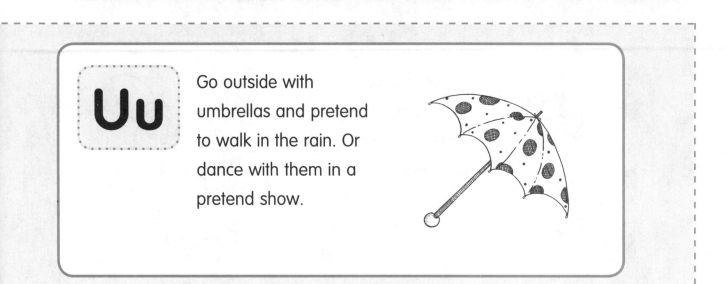

U u Play Up or Down: Give your child two objects that have clear "up" and "down" sides, such as plastic glasses. Have him or her place one in each hand. Then, in a manner similar to Simon Says, ask your child to turn the objects up or down. Increase the speed of the game until your child is confused.

U u Play Hide-and-Seek with the rule that the person hiding must hide under an object.

Vv Make vegetable soup for dinner.

Vv Make vests to wear around the house. You can use large paper bags from the grocery store for these by cutting up the front of the bag, then cutting holes for the head and arms. Your child can decorate the vests with markers and glue or with a variety of decorative papers.

Vv Create valentines for family members to let them know that they are loved (even when it is not Valentine's Day).

Make stained-glass windows out of wax paper. On a sheet of wax paper, place some crayon shavings. Place another sheet of wax paper on top and iron on a very low heat setting to melt the shavings and fuse the layers together. Be sure to protect the surface with newspapers or old towels before ironing. Cut the "stained glass" to size and place in your window.

On a windy day, make a wind chime. Tie common metal objects (discarded silverware, tin cans, jingle bells, old keys) on strings and group them in a tree so they touch when the wind blows.

Have waffles for breakfast. Or eat walnuts, watercress, or watermelon.

Make a W shape with your child by holding your hands overhead and standing close together. Or make a W shape using your fingers. Hold up the first and second fingers of both hands. Then overlap the first fingers to create the W shape. Trace this shape and post it on household objects that begin with the /w/ sound.

Xx Play Tic-Tac-Toe, letting your child be the one who draws the Xs.

Xx At snack time, cut small strips of cheese and form them into Xs on crackers.

Xx Draw pictures of people as they would appear on an X-ray (with only their bones showing).

Eat yogurt or yams. Pretend that the foods are "yucky," using appropriate facial expressions.

Celebrate Yellow Day! Dress in yellow, make a flower arrangement of yellow flowers (sunflowers or daisies work well), eat yellow food (such as eggs or cornbread), and color with crayons of various shades of yellow.

Make yarn paintings. Dip strands of yarn into paint and drag them across the paper.

Braid several strands of yarn to make friendship bracelets. Make them for family members or share them with friends.

Surprise your child by asking him or her to yell as loud as possible! Or create a family yell for your favorite sports team.

   Just-Right Homework Activities for PreK–K © 2009 by Diffily & Sassman, Scholastic Teaching Resources

 Create a pasta-and-vegetable dish using ziti and zucchini.

 Play a game of Zap! Starting in a "freeze" position, call out different actions that begin with the /z/ sound, such as "zip," "zoom," or "zigzag." Between each action, say "zap" to have players freeze in place.

Find all the zippers in the family's clothes.

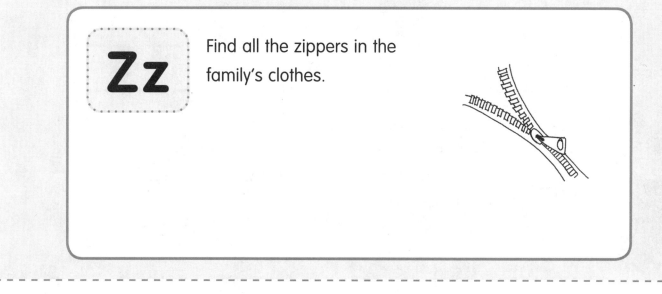

1
one

Ask your child to set the table with one fork, knife, spoon, plate, and so on at each person's place.

1
one

Eat one banana or one of some other item of food. Or serve one item of food to each family member.

1
one

Discuss how many items there are in one package; for example, a package of cookies.

1
one

Count the number of noses in your family. Help your child notice that there is one nose for each family member.

2
two

Make lists of things (write the words and have your child draw the objects) that come in twos: shoes, socks, eyes, hands, ears, arms, legs, bicycle tires, wings on a bird, and so on.

2
two

Collect coins and line them up in twos, counting each time "1, 2, 1, 2 . . ."

2
two

Working together with your child, go through a magazine or newspaper search for things that come in twos. Demonstrate how to page through the magazine, find an appropriate picture, cut it out, and glue it to an index card. On the back of the card, write the numeral 2.

3
three

Conduct a taste test using three foods. For example, place a small amount of three different cereals in three bowls. Taste each and describe the different tastes.

3
three

Help your child search the house to find things grouped in threes. Count the flowers in arrangements, the items on tables or shelves, and so on.

3
three

Make three-leaf clovers out of green construction paper.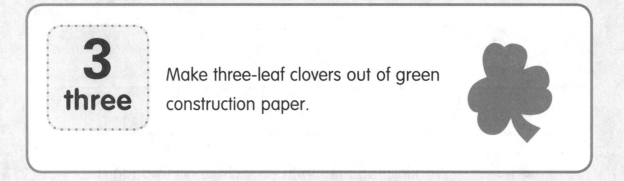

3
three

Retell the story of the "Three Little Bears." Help your child locate the appropriate props and use them in the retelling.

Just-Right Homework Activities for PreK–K © 2009 by Diffily & Sassman, Scholastic Teaching Resources

Make lists of things (write the words and have your child draw the objects) that come in fours: tires on a car, suits in a deck of cards, sides of a square (or rectangle or trapezoid), legs on a table, legs on a dog or cat, the primary directions (north, south, east, west), the four seasons (winter, spring, summer, fall), and so on.

Go through a deck of cards, sorting them into two piles: the ones that have a 4 on them and all the others.

Look through magazines and newspapers for the number 4 and circle them. Pay particular attention to how 4 appears in different fonts—sometimes the top is closed and sometimes it's open.

Place several small objects on the table. Ask your child to put them into groups of five. Then help him or her count the groups by fives. Pennies work well for this activity.

Make a "What Is Five?" poster. Using a large piece of paper, write the title at the top. Then challenge your child to draw appropriate things on the poster. Your child might trace his or her hand or draw a five-pointed star or a nickel.

Give your child five small objects, such as straws, toothpicks, or sticks. Ask him or her to arrange them in different ways. Then notice how the objects are grouped; for example, three might be closer to the right side than the other two. Comment on the different groupings that create a group of five.

 Just-Right Homework Activities for PreK–K © 2009 by Diffily & Sassman, Scholastic Teaching Resources

6
six

Make lists of things (write the words and have your child draw the objects) that come in sixes: soda cans or fruit juice six-packs, half of a dozen eggs, sides on dice, sides on boxes.

6
six

Go through a deck of cards, sorting them into two piles: the ones that have a 6 on them and all the others.

6
six

Count the legs on insects.

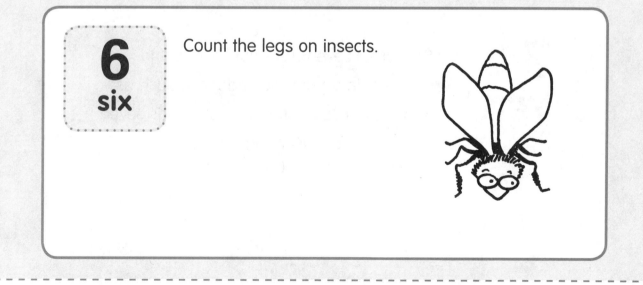

7
seven

Play Seven, Seven, Let's Do Seven. Tell your child to do seven repetitions of a motion, such as jumping seven times or walking seven paces.

7
seven

Roll play dough to create snakes that are exactly 7 inches long. If reading the ruler is difficult for your child, cut a strip of paper 7 inches long and use that to measure. After creating seven snakes, coil them to make a group of seven snakes!

7
seven

Play Search for Seven: Tell your child to find seven objects in a particular category, such as cans, bowls, or cups. After he or she finds seven objects, he or she must return them.

8
eight

Go through a deck of cards, sorting them into two piles: the ones that have an 8 on them and all the others.

8
eight

Count the sides of a stop sign.

8
eight

Count the tentacles on an octopus or the legs on a spider.

9
nine

Set a timer for nine minutes. Assign a task that can be completed in that length of time. Announce the passing of each minute.

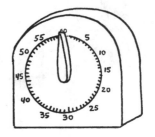

9
nine

Give your child some string and beads. Challenge him or her to string together nine beads. Have him or her wear the bead necklaces and count the number of beads for other family members.

9
nine

Use rubber stamps and inkpads to stamp pictures of nine objects. Put nine stamps together in a group. Use adding-machine tape or long strips of paper to stamp the pictures in a line.

Just-Right Homework Activities for PreK–K © 2009 by Diffily & Sassman, Scholastic Teaching Resources

 Go through a deck of cards, sorting them into two piles: the ones that have a 10 on them and all the others.

 Collect several books. Have your child look through each book and place a sticky note beside each 10.

 If you have a collection of pennies, use them to help your child count by 10s. First, count out 10 pennies and stack them. Repeat until you have 10 stacks. Then teach your child how to count by 10s: 10, 20, 30, 40, 50, 60, 70, 80, 90, 100.